LIBERIAN WOMEN
PEACEMAKERS

Fighting for the Right

To Be Seen, Heard

And Counted

A publication of the
African Women and Peace Support Group

Africa World Press, Inc.

P.O. Box 1892
Trenton, NJ 08607

P.O. Box 48
Asmara, ERITREA

Africa World Press, Inc.

P.O. Box 1892

Trenton, NJ 08607

P.O. Box 48

Asmara, ERITREA

www.africanworld.com

Book and Cover Design: Libby Bassett
Cover Photo: AP/Wide World Photo: Schalk van Zuydam

Library of Congress Cataloging-in-Publication Data

Liberian women peacemakers: fighting for the right to be seen, heard, and counted.
  120 p.   17.8 x 25.4 x .85 cm.
  ISBN 1-59221-251-4 (cloth) -- ISBN 1-59221-252-2 (pbk.)
  1. Liberia--History--Civil War, 1989---Women. 2. Liberia--Social conditions--1980- 3. Women and peace--Liberia. 4. Conflict management--Liberia. 5. Women--Liberia--Social conditions.

DT636.5.L528 2004
966.6203'3'082—dc22
                                                      2004002013

DEDICATION

We dedicate this small volume to the named and unnamed Liberian women who have risked their lives for the cause of peace. We hope it may help to make their peace activities and those of women across Africa and worldwide be seen, heard and counted.

TABLE OF CONTENTS

THE AFRICAN WOMEN AND PEACE SUPPORT GROUP

This publication is an African Women and Peace Support Group (AWPSG) project. We formed the group in 1997 to work with African women to document their peace efforts and increase recognition of their peace initiatives, especially among policy makers in various contexts and at all levels. This publication is the first of our efforts.

A group of Liberian women peace activists was identified by women and men, both in Liberia and outside it, who had been closely involved in peace processes during and following the first seven years of the conflict. The activists were interviewed by six Liberian journalists, and their interviews were compiled and interwoven for this publication. Brief biographies of the activists appear in Annex 1. The list of interviewers is found in Annex 2.

Most of the stories told and the quotes in the text are attributed. However, because these interviews took place only one or two years after the signing of the Abuja Peace Accord that brought that phase of the Liberian conflict to an end, there are occasions where sensitive quotes are not attributed. All quotations are from interviews unless otherwise identified.

The women and men interviewed are not intended to be a perfect research sample though they cover a range of ages, occupations, backgrounds, experiences and interventions. There are many more Liberian women with equivalent qualities and experiences who could have been interviewed, and we hope that their stories will appear elsewhere as documentation of women's peace efforts becomes more prevalent. The experiences reflected in this book largely represent those of Liberian women in Monrovia. Due to the inaccessibility of large parts of the country during the war, it was not possible to document as thoroughly the peace efforts of women in the countryside.

We worked closely with African women's groups, national and international non-governmental organizations (NGOs) and intergovernmental organizations to complete this study and ensure that women peacemakers are visible so they can have an impact on policy formulation and project development at all levels and in a variety of economic, political and social contexts.

> **COMFORT LAMPTEY**, Senior Advisor for Refugee Women, UNHCR, former Peace-building Advisor at UNIFEM after working with the NGO, International Alert, on conflict prevention and resolution

> **JANE MARTIN,** former Senior Program Officer, African American Institute; former Executive Director, U.S. Educational and Cultural Foundation in Liberia

> **CORANN OKORODUDU,** Professor of Psychology and African Studies, Rowan University; past President, Liberian Studies Association

> **GRETCHEN SIDHU,** Writer and Editor specializing in international development issues with intergovernmental organizations

> **MARGARET SNYDER**, founding Director of UNIFEM; Co-founder, African Centre for Women of the UN Economic Commission for Africa

> **MARGARET ADERINSOLA VOGT**, former Director, Africa Programme, UN International Peace Academy; currently Special Assistant to the Assistant Secretary-General, UN Department of Political Affairs

ACKNOWLEDGEMENTS

The African Women and Peace Support Group is most grateful to the Africa Bureau of the United Nations Development Programme (UNDP) and in particular to its assistant secretary-general at the time, Dr. Thelma Awori, for the project grant that financed country-level research, editorial and publication costs. Gender Adviser Viola Morgan was very helpful during implementation of the grant, which was provided through the UN Office for Project Services (UNOPS) represented by Binta Djibo, and managed by Friends of Liberia, a non-governmental organization. The views expressed in this volume do not necessarily reflect those of any UN agency or affiliated organization.

Medina Wesseh coordinated the work at field level, efficiently and tirelessly. The interviewers, despite constant civil unrest and thievery at their offices and homes, held intensive conversations with nearly 30 activists. We are profoundly grateful to all of them. We consulted frequently with Isha Dyfan of the International Women's Tribune Center and, during the initial stages of research, with Barbara Adams of the UN Non-Governmental Liaison Service. Theo Sowa produced the initial comprehensive manuscript. Libby Bassett edited and designed this book. Kassahun Checole and Angela Ajayi of Africa World Press, our publisher, have been fine cooperators.

We are most deeply grateful to all the Liberians, the men and women who gave their time and shared their stories of suffering, strategizing and demonstrating in their determined search to forge peace from chaos – and to the Liberian journalists who interviewed them.

CHRONOLOGY OF THE LIBERIAN CIVIL WAR
(1989-2003)

1989, Dec 24	The National Patriotic Front of Liberia (NPFL), led by Charles Taylor, attacks posts in Nimba County from Côte d'Ivoire, and President Doe responds by destroying towns and villages. The struggle is ignited.
1990, Jan	Inter-Faith Mediation Committee (IFMC) calls on Doe to resign.
1990, Jan-Jun	Citizens rally behind the call with marches, rallies, demonstrations. Independent Patriotic Front of Liberia (INPFL) splits from NPFL; civil war escalates.
1990, May	Economic Community of West African States (ECOWAS) establishes a Standing Mediation Committee to address the war.
1990, Jun 11-16	IFMC-initiated peace talks in Freetown, Sierra Leone, fail but provide model for ECOWAS efforts.
1990, Jul	Taylor and National Patriotic Front of Liberia close in on the capital, Monrovia, but Doe and his government remain in power.
1990, Aug 4	Taylor declares himself President of "Greater Liberia."
1990, Aug 24	ECOMOG (ECOWAS Monitoring Group) arrives in Monrovia.
1990, Aug 30	The Interim Government of National Unity (IGNU) formed in Banjul, The Gambia; Amos Sawyer elected interim president. NPFL does not participate. Women's organizations begin relief programs.
1990, Sep 9	Doe murdered by Prince Johnson of the Independent National Patriotic Front of Liberia (INPFL).
1990, Oct 10	Taylor sets up National Patriotic Reconstruction Assembly (NPRAG) as a government for "Greater Liberia."
1990, Fall	First Christian Health Association of Liberia (CHAL) workshop on reconciliation includes teachers, health workers, pastors.
1990, Nov 19	UN Security Council imposes arms embargo.
1990, Nov 21	Interim Government of National Unity installed in Monrovia.
1990, Nov 28	ECOWAS peace talks in Bamako, Mali; ceasefire fails to hold.

1991, Feb 12	ECOWAS peace conference in Lomé, Togo. Myrtle Gibson and Muna Wreh circulate a paper on women's concerns.
1991, Mar 15	Citizens organize First All Liberian Conference in Monrovia; results inconclusive.
1991, Apr	NPFL attacks Sierra Leone and Guinea for supporting ECOWAS; RUF in Sierra Leone benefits.
1991, Jun-Oct	ECOMOG is enlarged by addition of Senegalese and other troops. Four peace meetings take place in Yamoussoukro, Côte d'Ivoire; agreements reached on disarmament and encampments; "elections in six months" are never fulfilled.
1991, Oct	New ethnic-based factions – United Liberian Movement for Democracy (ULIMO) and Liberia United Defense Force (LUDF) – begin to fight against NPFL.
1991-1992	ULIMO gains NPFL territories.
1992, Apr 30	Military coup in Sierra Leone led by Victor Strasser, former ECOMOG officer in Liberia.
1992, Oct 20-1993, Jan	Operation Octopus – NPFL major offensive against Monrovia – is repulsed by ECOMOG forces.
1993	Factions increase and participate in war: Liberian Peace Council (LPC); Nimba Defense Council; ULIMO split: ULIMO-K (Kromah/Mandingo) and ULIMO-J (Johnson/Krahn).
1993, May 27	Carter Center's "Forum on Civic Education and Reconciliation" leads to the Liberian Network for Peace and Development (LNPD).
1993, Jul 25	A key agreement, the Cotonou Peace Accord, is signed, providing for a Liberian National Transitional Government (LNTG) to include faction representatives and civilians, and provisions for disarmament and elections.
1993, Sep 22	The United Nations Monitoring Group in Liberia (UNOMIL) is established.
1994, Feb 4	Founding meeting of the Liberian Women's Initiative (LWI), City Hall, Monrovia.
1994, Feb 10	First program and first position statement of the LWI.
1994, Mar 7	New LNTG officials are sworn in. Some factions are not included. Disagreements continue on allocation of ministries, disarmament.
1994, Apr	Carter Center reconciliation and conflict analysis workshop in Akosombo, Ghana, results in founding of Liberian Initiative for Peace Building and Conflict Resolution (LIPCORE).

1994, Sep 7	ECOWAS peace meetings, Akosombo. Civilians are excluded. NGOs and individuals deeply oppose the agreement.
1994, Oct	Second citizen-sponsored All-Liberia National Conference, Monrovia.
1994, Dec 21	ECOWAS peace meeting in Accra, Ghana. Terms are never effected. Women attend without invitation but finally receive official status.
1995, May 19	Meeting of ECOWAS Standing Mediation Committee at Abuja, Nigeria. Theresa Leigh-Sherman speaks on behalf of Liberian women.
1995, Jul	National Bank meeting in Monrovia: women's organizations hold four-day closed meeting with faction leaders.
1995, Aug 19	ECOWAS sponsors Abuja conference. Abuja I Agreement calls for complete ceasefire, demilitarization, plan for elections, collective presidency, movement of faction leaders to Monrovia.
1995, Aug	Second Liberian National Transitional Government (LNTG) is installed.
1995, end	ULIMO and NPFL fight against the Krahn-dominated Liberia Peace Council (LPC) in the interior.
1996, Jan	Mounting tensions among factions over the allocation of offices in the interim government.
1996, Apr 6	War is brought to Monrovia; ULIMO-K and NPFL attack ULIMO-J. Looting, destruction and killing continue in Monrovia; government of five-man council collapses and relief agencies leave.
1996, Jun	Gradual return of peace and relief organizations to Monrovia.
1996, Jul	ECOWAS Abuja meeting and Abuja II Peace Agreement. Ruth Perry appointed Head of State of third transitional government.
1997, Jul 19	Liberian national elections: Charles Taylor elected President. Ellen Johnson-Sirleaf of Unity Party comes in second in a field of 13 candidates.
1999	Liberians United for Reconciliation and Democracy (LURD) launches rebellion against Taylor in the north.
2000, May	Formation of Mano River Union Women's Peace Network (MARWOPNET).
2001, Mar	Security Council Resolution 1343 approves arms embargo, travel ban on government officials and other sanctions on Liberia.
	The Ministry of Gender and Development is established; Dorothy Musuleng Cooper is appointed as Minister.

2001, May 5	Thousands of women march to the UN office in Monrovia requesting international intervention in the conflict.
2002, Feb	Mano River Union Heads of State meet in Rabat, Morocco, and agree to work together to end cross-border insurgencies and promote peace.
2002, May 6	UN Security Council Resolution 1408 commends MAR-WOPNET and urges Liberian Government compliance with Resolution 1343 of March 7, 2001.
2003, Mar	A second rebel faction, Movement for Democracy in Liberia (MODEL), begins fighting in eastern Liberia.
2003, Mar 10	Women call on government and LURD to cease hostilities so that children can go to school and prepare to develop their country.
2003, Mar-Apr	A new women's organization, Women in Peace Building Network (WIPNET), and other women's organizations organize rallies and protests against the war.
2003, Apr 14	One thousand women stage peaceful assembly at Monrovia municipal office.
2003, Apr 15	Hundreds of white-clad women chant peace slogans and demand that government and rebel forces lay down arms.
2003, May	Women and other groups call for the immediate unconditional deployment of an international stabilizing force in the country.
2003, June	The two rebel groups control an estimated 80 percent of Liberia
2003, June 2	Hundreds of women stage anti-war demonstration in Monrovia; the Coalition of Women Political Parties calls for an international stabilization force.
2003, June 4	Peace talks begin in Accra, Ghana. A ceasefire is signed by President Taylor and the two rebel factions, LURD and MODEL, in Ghana but does not hold, and fighting continues.
	Charles Taylor is indicted by the International Criminal Court in Sierra Leone.
2003, Jun 17	Accra Ceasefire Agreement.
2003, Jun 18	One hundred women march to the U.S. Embassy calling for immediate and direct intervention by the U.S. Government.
2003, Aug 1	UN Security Council Resolution 1497 authorizes multinational force to assist implementation of the ceasefire.
2003, Aug 8	Emergency report is submitted to the UN Commission on Human Rights on international crimes and other gross violations of human rights committed in Liberia.

2003, Aug 11	Charles Taylor hands over power to his vice president, Moses Blah, and goes into exile in Calabar, Nigeria, following a Nigerian government arrangement.
2003, Aug 15	Liberian women at the talks set forth "The Golden Tulip Declaration," regarding inclusion of women in all existing and proposed institutions and structures of government.
2003, Aug 18	Ruth Perry chairs consultative meeting of Liberian women sponsored by MARWOPNET, UNIFEM and other organizations.
	The Comprehensive Peace Agreement (CPA) is signed among the warring parties in Accra under ECOWAS auspices.
2003, Sep 19	UN Security Council Resolution 1509 approves a UN mission in Liberia. (UNMIL) and up to 15,000 military personnel.
2003, Oct	West Africans become the first contingent of UN Peacekeepers.
2003, Oct 8	Liberia ratifies the UN Convention on the International Criminal Court.
2003, Oct 14	Installation of Gyude Bryant as interim President of Liberia.
2003, Dec 10	MARWOPNET is awarded the United Nations Prize in the Field of Human Rights, a prize given only every five years.

MAP OF LIBERIA

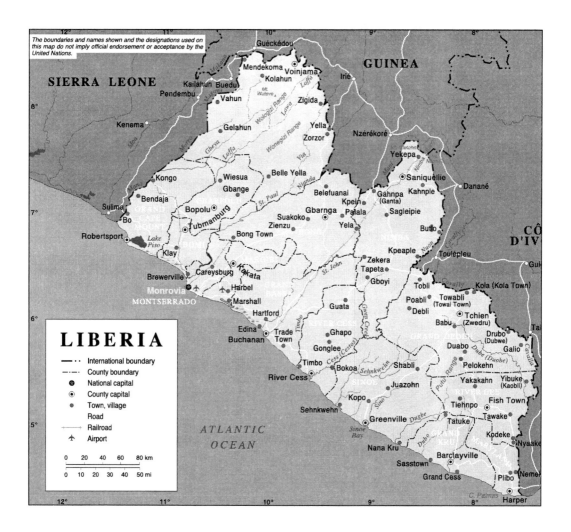

ACRONYMS

AFELL	Association of Female Lawyers of Liberia
AFL	Armed Forces of Liberia
AWAG	Abused Women and Girls Project (My Sister's Place)
AWCPD	African Women's Committee for Peace and Development
CAP	Child Assistance Program
CDC	Civic Disarmament Campaign
CEDE	Center for Democratic Empowerment
CHAL	Christian Health Association of Liberia
CPA	Comprehensive Peace Agreement
CUP	Churches United for Peace
CWO	Concerned Women's Organization
ECOMOG	ECOWAS Ceasefire Monitoring Group
ECOWAS	Economic Community of West African States
FAS	Femmes Afrique Solidarité
FERFAP	Federation of African Women's Peace Networks
IFMC	Inter-Faith Mediation Council
ICRC	International Committee of the Red Cross
IGNU	Interim Government of National Unity
INPFL	Independent National Patriotic Front of Liberia
JPC	Justice and Peace Commission
LCC	Liberian Council of Churches
LDF	Liberia Disarmament Fund
LIPCORE	Liberian Initiative for Peace and Conflict Resolution
LNC	Liberian National Conference
LNPD	Liberian Network for Peace and Development
LNTG	Liberian National Transitional Government
LPC	Liberia Peace Council
LPP	Liberian People's Party
LURD	Liberians United for Reconciliation and Democracy
LWI	Liberian Women's Initiative
MARWOPNET	Mano River Union Women Peace Network
MODEL	Movement for Democracy in Liberia
MOJA	Movement for Justice in Africa
NAEAL	National Adult Education Association of Liberia
NAWOCOL	National Women's Commission of Liberia
NGLS	Non-Governmental Liaison Service (UN)
NMCL	National Muslim Council of Liberia
NPFL	National Patriotic Front of Liberia (Charles Taylor faction)
OAU	Organization of African Unity

RUF	Revolutionary United Front (Sierra Leone)
RWA	Rural Women's Association
SELF	Special Emergency Life Food Programme
SRSG	Special Representative of the UN Secretary-General
ULIMO	United Liberation Movement of Liberia for Democracy
ULIMO-J	United Liberation Movement of Liberia for Democracy–Johnson
ULIMO-K	United Liberation Movement of Liberia for Democracy–Kromah
UNDP	United Nations Development Programme
UNECA	United Nations Economic Commission for Africa
UNHCR	United Nations High Commission for Refugees
UNICEF	United Nations Children's Fund
UNIFEM	United Nations Development Fund for Women
UNMIL	United Nations Mission in Liberia
UNOMIL	United Nations Observer Mission to Liberia
USAID	United States Agency for International Development
WIPNET	Women in Peace Building Network
WODAL	Women's Development Association of Liberia
WOUPAD	Women United for Peace and Development

FOREWORD

Today, more than ever before, there is clear acknowledgment the world over of the consequences of wars on women's lives and of the immense contributions that women can and do make towards building peace and security.

After the Cold War ended, the changing nature of warfare was quickly evident in the tide of new conflicts that have erupted, most of them internal with unprecedented levels of civilian casualties.

Against this backdrop, civil society groups in war-torn countries have been very vocal in calling for changes in the rules and conventions that inform processes of negotiation and peace-building, in order to ensure that those most adversely affected are included in all efforts to create peace. Women's voices have been prominent in this respect. Whether at national, regional or global levels, women mobilize to highlight the negative impacts of wars on their own and their children's lives. They also advocate for recognition of, and support for, their efforts to build peace and demand that women be represented at all stages of formal peace processes – from negotiations to post-conflict reconstruction.

The calls of women are slowly being heard. One of the clearest demonstrations of this positive response is the adoption by the United Nations Security Council of Resolution 1325, in October 2000. The Resolution acknowledges the impact of armed conflicts on women and calls for increased support to enhance their contributions to peace-building processes. Since its adoption, a number of important UN and NGO publications have addressed the subject and offered practical recommendations for protecting women in armed conflict situations and strengthening their roles as agents of peace.

In many countries and regions affected by war, women's peace networks are working tirelessly to inform processes for building sustainable peace. The African continent, disproportionately affected by the recent wave of internal armed conflicts, has witnessed the emergence of women-led peace initiatives and networks, including regional networks such as the African Women's Committee for Peace and Development (AWCPD), the Federation of African Women's Peace Networks (FERFAP) and the Mano River Union Women's Peace Network (MARWOPNET). At the national level, this includes organizations such as the Sudanese Women's Voice for Peace, IIDA Women's Development Association in Somalia, the Liberia Women's Initiative, the Sierra Leone Women's Forum and the consortium of Burundian and

Congolese women who are working to inform the peace negotiations in their respective countries.

The African Women and Peace Support Group, which initiated this publication, was born in 1997 at the height of the period of activism with calls by African women to increase their leadership in peace efforts. The support group, made up of six African women and friends of Africa, sought to record the wealth of knowledge, experience and strategies that women have employed to advance peace efforts on the continent, and as a first step, undertook to document the experiences of Liberian women. When they approached me as Assistant Administrator and Director of the Regional Bureau for Africa at the United Nations Development Programme, I jumped at the chance to partner with them in paying homage to the women of Liberia. I commend the support group for giving the Liberian women their well-deserved place in history.

This book details Liberian women's peace activities from the onset of the civil war in 1989 up until the elections of 1997 – a period when these women had little time or space to reflect on or document their initiatives. It presents highlights of their action thereafter, until the peace agreement of 18 August 2003. It conveys the rich and complex experiences of women in their own words and vividly illustrates the countless and diverse ways in which they sought to influence the peace process. For these women, the task of building peace was a multi-faceted process, ranging from addressing the humanitarian needs of their communities for food, water, shelter and health care, to facilitating dialogue among members of the various warring factions, to demanding and obtaining a hearing at the peace negotiations table.

It is precisely at this most challenging moment – as a transitional government and an international peacekeeping force work for stability – that a clear testament, which depicts women's past achievements and challenges in building peace, is most urgently desired. This historical account will continue to remind Liberian women of their past accomplishments and bolster and encourage their ongoing peace efforts.

For women in war-affected countries in the rest of Africa and beyond, this publication provides a useful reference from which to draw inspiration and lessons to inform their own efforts at building peace. For the general public, including donors, international organizations and policy-makers, this publication represents an important addition to the existing body of knowledge that enhances our understanding of the political and development transition of Liberia.

Moreover, by stressing the contributions of women to the peace process, this book serves as a tool for advocacy to increase attention and support to women's ongoing initiatives and to ensure that their numerous informal contributions to peace processes are both acknowledged and rewarded. Above all, it should impel us to heed the long-standing pleas of women in conflict areas, to give them a voice and an opportunity to be equally represented in leadership and decision-making at all stages of peace processes that affect their lives.

THELMA AWORI
Former Assistant Administrator
and Director of the Africa Bureau
United Nations Development Programme

A woman protesting for peace cries out in front of United Nations headquarters in Monrovia, asking the UN to stop the killing, rape, torture and looting in Liberia.

AP/Wide World Photo: Pewee Flomoku

Part I:
THE 1989-1997 CIVIL WAR AND WOMEN

INTRODUCTION

The civil war of 1989-1997 and the fighting that renewed soon after, lasting until the peace agreement of August 18, 2003, affected every area of Liberia, every village and town, and every family. It was a terrifying experience. When its stories are told, women are described as victims of sexual and other physical violence, and sometimes praised for protecting children, healing families and maintaining communities. But when conflict or conflict resolution and peace-building are the focus of discussions, women are almost invariably trivialized or left completely invisible. Their absence from peace tables and other political negotiations fails to acknowledge their initiatives in a whole range of peace processes.

This publication focuses on that seldom-documented aspect of the conflict – the impact of women on peace initiatives and processes during and after the war. Women, victims themselves, fought for peace, pleading with young soldiers not to kill, to lay down their guns, and to allow convoys of food to go through their checkpoints to the hungry. As the months and years passed, with no peace in sight, they gained strength together, took to the streets in protest, and eventually stormed men's peace conferences to speak plainly and forcefully about the destruction of families, communities and the nation.

The story of Liberian women's roles during the war – like those of women in conflict situations everywhere – is complex. It is not simply that all women worked for peace while men waged war. There were women who fought and women who by their actions opted to continue the war, and there were many men who worked for peace.

While recognizing that reality, this book gives voice to some of the many thousands of women who were prepared to risk their lives to defy the abuse, face their attackers, remember their traditions and take an active stand for peace. It highlights women's collective peacemaking and peace-building efforts and is a celebration of their commitment, imagination, expertise and courage. It describes both their successes and their challenges and shows that, despite many hurdles, women did make a difference in efforts to end the war in Liberia. Their story deserves to be told.

To place the story in context, we begin with a brief history.

A BRIEF HISTORY OF LIBERIA AND THE CIVIL WAR

Liberia was founded in 1816 as a place of resettlement for freed North American slaves and became an independent republic in 1847. Between 1847 and 1980 its politics and economics were dominated to a large extent by those settlers and their descendents. Issues of inequitable access and opportunity and outright discrimination became a focus of resentment that came to a head in the 1980 coup d'etat led by Sergeant Samuel Doe. His bloody coup was the precursor of a political reign characterized by corruption, violence and economic decline.

Explanations of the causes of the conflict have focused on political and socio-economic conditions in the 1980s and sometimes on earlier institutionalized inequities. However, the December 1989 incursions by Charles Taylor's National Patriotic Front of Liberia (NPFL) into parts of northeastern Liberia, are generally seen as the start of the violent internal conflict that was to engulf the nation and its citizens between 1990 and 1996. The conflict was marked by terrifying levels of brutality by all factions against civilian populations, the destruction of Liberia's social and economic infrastructure; the kidnapping, recruitment and abuse of children as soldiers and the destruction of civilian political authority.

Exact figures are not available, but during the first conflict, fought by several warring factions over those initial seven years, an estimated 150,000 Liberians were killed, many in brutal massacres. By 2003, according to United Nations statistics, the numbers had risen to 250,000 possibly killed and more than a half million driven into exile out of a total population of 3.3 million. Although no one really knows the numbers, everyone can name people who died. And everyone has a tale of sorrow, struggle and courage to tell.

During the years 1989 to 1997, the focus of this chapter, Liberians lived in an uncertain world that vacillated between war and a fragile calm. The first months were among the most terrifying: food disappeared and the nation's infrastructure was destroyed. As new factions developed and took up arms against each other, life for citizens in the interior of the country grew increasingly dangerous. The fighters were not trained soldiers but large numbers of young boys, some as young as eight years, and men who joined for adventure or, more often, to avenge killings of kin and townspeople, to protect their communities from factions or because they were given an ultimatum: join or be killed. They defied and defiled traditions, held people hostage, raped and tortured women and children, murdered at will. Many were said to be on drugs.

A significant number of young girls were captured and were victims of atrocious acts of rape and other gender-based violence. While most of the girls did not take part in actual combat, they served as bush wives to the combatants – cooking, carrying loads and being sex slaves, often to multiple partners. Many became pregnant and bore children of the fighters.

The first six months of the conflict saw escalating levels of violence inflicted on civilian populations throughout the country, culminating in a battle for the capital, Monrovia, in the summer of 1990. In that battle the Armed Forces of Liberia (AFL), the Independent National Patriotic Front (INPFL) and NPFL forces embarked on a killing spree of innocent civilians. This included random killings of individuals, the massacre of more than 600 civilians, mainly women and children, in the UN compound, at St. Peter's Lutheran Church and in the USAID compound in Monrovia, and the murder by burning of 200 women and children in the Sinkor Supermarket. The Economic Community of West African States (ECOWAS) monitoring group, ECOMOG, finally drove the rebel forces out of the city. It has been estimated that more than 60,000 civilians were killed in Monrovia alone between July and November 1990. Tens of thousands more were injured.

As the conflict progressed, development efforts in rural and urban areas were devastated. The armed violence diminished traditional governance structures and destroyed communal activities. More immediate was the worsening humanitarian situation: spiraling rates of disease and severe malnutrition were problems throughout the country, but particularly in urban centers where there was little access to the agricultural produce available in some rural areas. Monrovia, with its ECOMOG soldiers, was a comparatively safe haven through much of the war, excepting the period July to November 1990 described above, October 1992 to early 1993 when the NPFL launched Operation Octopus against the city, and the months of April and May 1996 when the factions living there fought each other, killed civilians and devastated the city.

> Can you imagine going through something like 50 and more checkpoints and the interrogations, traveling from Gbarnga to Monrovia? ... Those are some of the serious risks we took just to bring peace to our beloved country. You keep talking whether people want to listen or not. You just keep talking. Sometimes insults are hurled at you simply because of the area you come from. But you have to keep talking peace.
> *Serena Galawolo, Concerned Women of Greater Liberia*

Throughout the war, the main artery for access throughout the country – between Gbarnga (NPFL headquarters) in the northeast and Monrovia – was closed to most traffic, and whoever commanded Gbargna commanded the interior and even the coasts, since the main road branches to east and west at Gbargna with feeder roads toward the coast. The few vehicles still moving were delayed at the very frequently placed checkpoints where soldiers demanded "your goods or your money" and could kill if you did not comply or spoke the wrong language. People who fled from east and west walked and, if lucky, used wheelbarrows along safer routes through forest and bush paths to reach markets or refugee camps.

Human devastation

In short, everyone had reason to fear. Fighters might come by day or night for food or to kill and burn homes because they suspected the residents of sup-

porting enemy factions. Survival was the issue. It was a struggle to plant or harvest after men who usually cleared the land were killed or recruited. Chickens, pigs, goats, dogs disappeared, and people relied on wild fruits and cabbage from the palm tree for food. Markets shrank or disappeared, and most roads deteriorated so badly that when the first peace came in 1996-1997 government and relief agencies had to use sea routes to reach coastal towns and to hack their way through the undergrowth and trees so that trucks might pass inland.

The terrorizing of civilian populations resulted in huge numbers of refugees and displaced families. Those fleeing their homes made their way to six major displaced persons centers within the country. They met Sierra Leoneans fleeing the war in their own country when they walked or rode across the borders to relatives or to refugee camps. By 1995, the United Nations High Commission for Refugees (UNHCR) estimated that more than 850,000 Liberians were refugees in neighboring

In a devastated village "no time for war."

West African states – Côte d'Ivoire, Guinea, Sierra Leone, Ghana and Nigeria – while over one million – nearly another third of the country's population – were internally displaced as a result of the conflict. Families were often separated by the war, although the International Committee of the Red Cross (ICRC) and, much later on, a local radio station, Star Radio, made special efforts to reunite them. Some will never learn what happened to their loved ones.

The ECOWAS peacekeeping force, ECOMOG (consisting mainly of Nigerian and Ghanaian troops) arrived in August 1990 and was involved in the conflict in various ways for the next seven years. ECOMOG managed to operate, with varying degrees of success, in extremely difficult conditions – constantly changing social, economic and political environments, insufficient funds to pay for the larger, stronger and more comprehensive peacekeeping mission that was needed, and slow and marginal support from the international community.[1]

The carnage continued despite attempts at diplomatic cessation of the violence through the interventions of civil society groups as well as the diplomatic and physical interventions of ECOWAS, the United Nations and other international actors following the collapse of the state and the prevailing anarchy. Those organizations recognized first an Interim Government of National Unity (IGNU), and, later, Liberian National Transitional Governments (LNTGs) instituted as a result of the Cotonou (1993) and Abuja I (1995) peace accords.

The 1989-97 conflict was marked by 46 political mediation meetings, ceasefire agreements and peace accords involving warring factions with national and international participants, often under ECOWAS auspices. Over a dozen peace agreements were signed. These failed attempts were often followed by surges in the violence engulfing the country. The Abuja II peace agreement of 1996 brought a fragile peace, elections and a new government under President Charles Taylor in July 1997. This chapter, Part I, covers this period, 1989-1997, while 1998-2003 appears in Part II.

The breakdown of civil life: women's views

Women, forced to watch their husbands and sons killed, tortured and kidnapped, were subjected to unspeakable acts of violence on their persons and against their children while attempting to sustain the vestiges of their families and communities. Former presidential candidate and political activist Ellen Johnson-Sirleaf describes some of the effects of the savage violence:

> It wasn't so much the physical destruction, it was the change in values, the change in attitudes...the disregard for life, for rights, for due process, for others.... And this came...from rather decent people [who] over the years had developed it. I think it was an attitude best described as one of hopelessness and despair, with no real promise and hope for the future. People just concentrated on "how do you survive today" – by any means possible, no matter what it means. [Even] if it meant the infringement of someone else's life and liberty – your survival was it.

---

[1] ECOMOG's involvement in the conflict produced accusations of partiality, corrupt behavior by some of the troops and occasions where ECOMOG itself was viewed as one of the parties to the conflict rather than a peacekeeping entity. Despite these shortcomings and some setbacks, ECOMOG activity undoubtedly provided increased protection and security for large parts of the civilian population, reduced potential levels of violence and arguably was one of the elements that shortened the protracted armed conflict.

The other thing that was very shocking was…the total abandon-
ment of rural life. Rural life traditionally in Liberia could be better
than urban life. People kept their villages clean, they provided their
own sustenance through their own effort. They sometimes lacked
the social services to which they were entitled, but they lived rela-
tively well. Then, all of a sudden there were abandoned villages,
people living on the fringes, or close to urban centers – again, as a
matter of survival. It was very heartbreaking. The very *moral* fiber
of the nation, the glue that held us together, with all of our problems and difficulties – that seemed to have been broken apart by the
years of military rule followed by so many years of civil strife.

Her comments are reflected in the demographic statistics available that cover
the time of the conflict. In 1974, 29 percent of the Liberian population lived
in urban areas. In 1999, that proportion had risen to 46 percent. Gross domestic product dropped from U.S.$973 million in 1987 to U.S.$396 million in
1999 while the country's debt burden per capita rose from $373 in 1980, to
$700 in 1989 to $1160 in 1999. The 1999 Human Development Report found
national unemployment at 80 percent, with 85 percent of the population living below the poverty line and 55 percent living in "absolute poverty,"
Female illiteracy was running at 81 percent.

It is against this background of social, economic, political and military chaos
that civil society groups in Liberia initiated a variety of peace activities,
including diplomatic, political, humanitarian and community peace-building.
Women were involved in many of these activities as leaders of civil society
groups, as key advisors to social and political organizations, and as founders,
activists and workers in women's groups that were often formed specifically
to deal with the conflict.

PEACE-BUILDING ACTIVITIES

Women: survivors, providers and healers

Women's roles extended throughout the process. From day one
actually, as I recall, women's concern about the war and the conditions leading to the war were very well known. They may not have
been organized in the kinds of fashion we see them organized
today, but we know prior to the war, either in collaboration with,
or…as part of the Liberia Council of Churches, women were
involved.

Former Head of State Amos Sawyer

The experience of women during the civil war is a story of courage and hope,
amid great pain and suffering. Women had always played important roles in

Liberian society as farmers, marketers, politicians, lawmakers, entrepreneurs, managers, special elders (*zoes*), members and leaders in religious and other civil society organizations, and as mothers in charge of large and complex households. Yet fighters showed them no regard. During the war they were tortured, *tarbayed* (tied with elbows meeting behind their backs), strip searched at will and, of course, raped and otherwise sexually violated.

A limited survey carried out by women health workers in 1994[2] indicates that nearly half of the women interviewed had experienced at least one act of physical or sexual violence by a combatant. As one woman commented, "Women were treated like geese that were battered."[3] Some women exchanged their bodies for food to help families stay alive. Others of all ages were raped in the course of being forced to cook for soldiers or when they were intentionally targeted. Citizens were lined up to watch murders and rapes – even those of their loved ones. As younger women left villages and towns, or escaped their captors, older women, even mothers, were raped by young boys – an outrage toward those to whom all were expected to give respect.[4]

A Liberian aid worker with a poster aimed at preventing rape and violence, displayed at a center for women in the refugee camp at the Samuel K. Doe Stadium in Monrovia.

Although women suffered, they also triumphed. The war forced them to take on new roles. "If rebels killed your husband, what could you do?" one reflected. Drawing on their experience of running large households, they opened their homes to provide for families and homeless war victims who sometimes numbered more than 30 in one residence. They had always been mediators, interceders and negotiators, and usually made the rules for the family – activities that would stand them in good stead during the war. Whether they remained in Liberia or fled to refugee camps, women devised ways to do marketing, and they started small shops and businesses. In Côte d'Ivoire and Ghana a number of Liberian refugee women learned carpentry and masonry and built houses as part of a UNIFEM program.

---

[2] Swiss, Shana, Peggy J. Jennings, Gladys V. Aryee, Grace H. Brown, Ruth M. Jappah-Samukai, Mary S. Kamara, Rosana D.H. Schaack, Rojatu S. Turay-Kanneh, "Violence Against Women During the Liberian Civil Conflict," *Journal of the American Medical Association*, February 25, 1998, Vol. 279, No. 8.

[3] Bennett, Olivia, Jo Bexley and Kitty Warnock, Eds., *Arms to Fight, Arms to Protect: Women Speak Out About Conflict,* Panos Publications, 1996, p. 36.

[4] Turshen, Meredith, and Clotilde Twagiramariya, *What Women Do in Wartime*, New York: Zed Books, Ltd., 1998, pp.132-133.

Ruth Caesar recalls heroic individual actions:

> I remember Julia who was a university student, and her parents got
> separated from her and the family and she had to support her little
> brothers. She sold [in the] market, she braved bullets and went to
> the villages to buy produce to bring to the market all through the
> war. I think she is a peacemaker; she is a heroine. Then there were
> the elderly women like TG, who would sit on her own porch where
> she was displaced and beckon to people that were passing by, give
> them… encouraging words, telling them to hold on, telling them to
> keep the faith. She [had] lost everything – she's also a heroine.
> There are several women in that category.

This spirit overflowed into the political arena, and women took the lead in
demanding peace. Their new determination is described in the 1994 Position
Statement on the Liberian War of their peace-centered organization, The
Liberian Women's Initiative (LWI)[5]:

> We, the women of Liberia, are the mothers of the land. We feel the
> joys and sorrows of this land in a special way because we are
> women. Not only do we represent one half of the population, but
> we also feel a special sense of responsibility for our children, our
> husbands and our brothers who make up the other half of the pop-
> ulation. We take care of the society. We soothe the pains. We are the
> healers and peacemakers. We call on all women of Liberia at home
> and abroad to unite and join our efforts in aiding the peace process
> in Liberia clear its final hurdle. The struggle for survival as a nation
> and as a people is presently at a delicate and crucial stage. For the
> past four years, we have been killed, raped, starved to death, mis-
> used and abused. We have witnessed the horror of having our chil-
> dren, our husbands, our fathers and other relatives killed and
> maimed before our very eyes. We have experienced starvation to
> the point of becoming walking skeletons. We have been stripped of
> our dignity as human beings! The women have borne all of this vic-
> timization with suffering and stoic silence. This silence is not to be
> construed as weakness or acquiescence.

Basic needs: food, shelter and healing the trauma

From the beginning of the civil war many women responded directly to the
needs of their neighbors and communities, and to strangers who, like themselves, were caught up in violent and devastating conflict. Some of their "tra-

---

5 The Liberian Women's Initiative, *Position Statement on the Liberian Civil War*. Monrovia,
1994, p. 1, as quoted in Doris H. Railey, "Some Impacts of the Liberian Civil War: A Pilot
Study of Thirty Liberian Immigrant Families in the United States," *Liberian Studies Journal*, XXII, 2, 1997, p. 261.

ditional" actions became fraught with risks not previously experienced, but they were willing and able to transcend customary boundaries and move beyond safe havens. Amos Sawyer, first interim president of Liberia, explains:

> The roles played by women in the preservation of lives, the suste-nance of lives during the war were unprecedented in this society. It was women who were going out finding the food, keeping the chil-dren safe, and in many instances...hiding the men from danger.

Almost immediately after the Interim Government was established in 1990, women began to join together to develop organizations to help war victims. "For the first two or three years, our concentration was on relief," says Etwe-da Cooper. For example:

The Special Emergency Life Food Programme (SELF) exemplifies the many groups that were not exclusively women's organizations but in which women played key roles. Dorothea Diggs was the coordinator of SELF, which organ-ized food distribution systems for international relief during the chaotic peri-od of the early 1990s that was marked by massive displacement and the sub-sequent relocation of individuals, families and communities. SELF assisted communities to approach food distribution as a method of peace-building rather than as a scarce resource that could increase divisions. Getting the food to those who needed it was risky and dangerous. Diggs states:

> When the ship got here we were feeding directly from the Freeport [docking area in Monrovia] straight out to communities because people were really dying. And there was nothing. We lived only on tea in Monrovia. Going out and working with the fighters at the Freeport was peace-building because my life was involved.... Later on we became friendly with [the fighters], but when they wanted food, I couldn't give them [any] as long as they were holding guns.

Although shy at first, women became community team leaders as the system evolved. Diggs says they played crucial roles in the face of extreme food shortages and conflict:

> We got community people involved. Those communities were mapped, we blocked up each area...and they would take down names and household and bring them to us.... If you take three, four bags of rice for your own, how do I report it? We give the food to the community and the community is supposed to share it. Sometimes they would forfeit it, because this man and myself had fuss [disagreement], so your whole family will not eat just because of that.... It was hard – the people still couldn't agree to forgiving people.... Many times I had to go in the community and talk and then take extra food to some family because the community did not share with them.

Women also helped people return to their destroyed villages to rebuild their lives and their homes. Hawa Goll Kotchi observes:

> It's talking to people and just trying to help them find food, to help them to find seedlings for their farm, help them to put up shelters because all the houses were broken. So what they did was the few, the two or three houses that were standing, the first batch of people went back, and they all lived in these two or three houses while they worked and helped the other people to build their houses. But it's a difficult thing when you have persons in the village who have watched their colleagues, people they grew up with…watched them being killed. It takes a lot of courage.

Children eat their ration of rice and beans in meat soup at the UNICEF-supported Good Samaritan Orphanage for abandoned or orphaned children in Mamba Point, Monrovia.

The capital city, where thousands of families from the countryside found shelter, was the focus of myriad relief efforts. For example, in 1991, a group of Muslim women opened the United Muslim Women's Education and Day Care Center in Monrovia to cater to children displaced or unable to attend school as a result of the conflict. The center had to close down during the violent military activity of Operation Octopus but reopened in 1993, when a home for abandoned children was added.

Their response to the vicious Operation Octopus attack on Monrovia, launched by NPFL in October 1992, showed that women could organize and cross fighting lines more easily than men. As the fighting involved new factions countrywide, particularly the United Liberation Movement of Liberia for Democracy (ULIMO), women played leading roles in maintaining communication. Groups such as Concerned Women of Liberia, Women in Action for Good Will, the Muslim Women's Federation and older groups such as Women's Development Association of Liberia (WODAL), the Federation of Liberian Women and the umbrella organization, The National Women's Commission of Liberia (NAWOCOL), supported whole communities affected by the conflict through food distribution, care for displaced and refugee families, and healing and reconciliation workshops.

When ULIMO forces captured Kakata in 1992, they blocked the flow of traffic, services and goods along the route from Gbarnga to Monrovia. Hearing of acute food shortages in the capital, the Concerned Women's Organization (CWO) held meetings with their Monrovia and Gbarnga chapters and local market women to develop a joint plan to deliver food to Monrovia. The women traders mobilised others and gathered quantities of foodstuffs for transport, then negotiated a safe passage with NPFL forces in Gbarnga, which allowed them to cross checkpoints. But when they reached Kakata they faced young ULIMO soldiers with guns pointed at them. Following several hours of intense negotiations about the humanitarian nature of their mission and ECOMOG intervention, ULIMO allowed the women passage. In addition to negotiating some 50 checkpoints they had to cope with roads that had been devastated by the conflict, slowing progress of the journey considerably. Arriving in Monrovia at last, they held a food sale at CWO headquarters. The courage and solidarity of their northern sisters – working across faction lines – is still well remembered by the women of Monrovia, says Serena Galawolo:

> Foodstuffs that could not be found in Monrovia for more than seven months were all brought down by us, the women from Gbarnga. We brought palm oil, bitter balls, pepper. We brought whole lots of foodstuffs from the rural areas and sold them for very little prices that most people could afford to buy.

Also in 1992, a group of women who had been displaced by the fighting in Monrovia two years earlier returned to establish the Feeding, Literacy and Recreation Project under the auspices of the YMCA. That year they worked with over 500 underprivileged, war affected children between the ages of five and 12, providing regular meals, trauma counseling, recreational activities and basic literacy programs.

Psychological healing

Psychological healing, often through trauma counseling also was essential for survival and to create an environment for peace-building. Women in Action for Goodwill, which solicited relief items and distributed them to women and children in displaced persons and refugee camps, added trauma counseling for women and children to their activities.

Evelyn Kandakai tells of her involvement in peacemaking through the National Adult Education Association Peace Education Program:

> We sponsored programs to talk about peace, to encourage Liberians to get into the need for peace. One of our strategies was awareness building. We had what we called a Peace Education Extravaganza, and a Children's Peace Festival. We involved schools... nursery schools and children from other areas outside of schools....

> We took a peace theater from the Kendeja Cultural Center. With
> UNICEF assistance we were able to organize a peace education and
> resource center.... We were one of the groups that brought about
> the environment for people to want to sing about peace, to talk
> about peace, to get involved in peace education and peacemaking.

At "Our Sister's Place," NOWOCOL and UNICEF offered the Abused
Women and Girls (AWAG) program. One woman interviewed for this study,
Tonia Wiles, indicated that a thousand women and girls had been helped at
AWAG by counselors and lawyers, including members of the Association of
Female Lawyers of Liberia (AFELL).

Sessions on conflict resolution and reconciliation for groups of religious leaders and professionals such as doctors, nurses and teachers were organized by
the Christian Health Association of Liberia (CHAL) from 1990 throughout
the war and up to the present day. Elizabeth Mulbah recalls:

> I remember when we started our round of healing and reconcilia-
> tion workshops to bring people together. The first thing, they did-
> n't want to even sit near each other. They did not want to speak to
> one another. But by the fifth day some were able to tell others "I am
> sorry." They were shaking hands. They were hugging and they
> were crying.

Advocacy: mediation and networking

Advocacy in support of peace embraced work with national and international actors: senior diplomats and UN officials, faction members and leaders,
civil society groups and a range of grass roots activists in communities.
Women used mediation and networking as their initial tools. Many of them
mediated on their own – often at great personal risk – with political actors
involved in the conflict and with individuals and communities affected by it.
They sought to build bridges to the many separate warring factions, initially
with varied levels of success.

One woman, who did not want to be identified, was not part of any civil society or women's organization in 1993. Working through an old school friend
who had become part of a particular faction, she managed to establish contact
with its leader. The same woman was the conduit through which links were
later established between women's organizations and the faction that she had
dissuaded from entering Monrovia:

> Somebody came to me and said that the [faction] was committing
> a lot of atrocities in the Greenville area. I don't know what made
> me think that I could talk them out of anything, but I tried. So I met

these men, I asked them for an audience. They agreed, they came,
we sat there and we talked and talked. I tried to convince them that
if they decided to come into Monrovia – can they imagine the
atrocities? Finally [their leader] said okay they were not going to
come to Monrovia as they had said they would to pursue Taylor.

Clara d'Almeida was part of a private advocacy initiative determined to per-
suade combatants to surrender their guns in return for finding them civilian
employment. She discovered a group of armed combatants on her doorstep at
midnight who wanted to continue discussions started earlier. She tells her
story of that encounter:

I don't know how they found my house, but one of the men
knocked on my door. He was a frontline commander. I said, "Who
is that?" and he said "I'm so and so." I said, "So and so? How did
you find my house?" He said "There is nowhere in Monrovia we
can't find if we want to.... We trust you; that is why we came
here. We have other frontline commanders here, and we want to
talk to you." I got up, put on my blue jeans and said to myself,
"You can't act scared, you've got to act brave." We sat on the
porch and we talked, and they told me where they were coming
from, what they intended to do. So we met them halfway and they
produced. I mean a good amount of them gave up the guns and
came to town.

In the course of gathering and selling produce in rural and urban areas,
women market traders had contact with many faction leaders and combatants.
These women had powerful and effective networks for acting as mediators
between larger groups of women and faction leaders at various points in the
conflict. Says Annie Saydee, Governor of Sapo:

We talked to them [the faction leaders]. They are children to us, and
we wanted this fighting to stop. We the women…bear that pain. So
we begged them – Kromah, Boley, Taylor – at different times.

They and other concerned women spoke personally to combatants and faction
leaders at community and national levels in attempts to begin negotiations for
peace. Such individual meetings often had encouraging short-term effects
including, for example, the reopening of the Gbarnga-Monrovia road for
goods and services. Perhaps even more important were the longer-term
impacts that arose from relationships of trust established between women's
groups and faction leaders and the sense of action, determination and control
of events that such mediation imparted to the women's peace movement.

Such networking can be credited for some of the more successful advocacy
actions. At community and national levels women used their personal con-

tacts with civil society organizations, members of varying factions, religious and professional affiliations, kinship ties and old friendships as well as knowledge of and involvement in food distribution and marketing chains, and any other links they could leverage. They facilitated information exchange, consultation and strategic planning for both humanitarian actions and political advocacy. Peace activist and businesswoman Etweda Cooper links the range of networking to the range of women involved in peace initiatives:

> There were a lot of people involved in this peace process.... We had lawyers, doctors, marketers, very educated women, unemployed women, women who worked with the UN, women who were illiterate.

A "grapevine" information system enabled women's organizations to plan meetings, consultations or demonstrations with a few hours' notice, bypassing the media when it was expedient or when there were no funds to pay for it. In the words of economist and civil servant Ruth Caesar:

> We established a simple information system where if one community got the information on a meeting or a march…before two to three hours the other communities would have been mobilized. We could call a meeting in maybe half a day and get 75 or 80 persons. We had in place [something] like roadrunners, where information traveled because most of the time we did not have money to pay for the press, newspaper or other media, and there were times when we did not feel like going to the press. We just used the grapevine to get our messages across.

Networking with the world

As advocacy initiatives advanced, the networks reached far beyond national borders. Contacts with diaspora Liberians were exploited to keep issues of peace in Liberia on the agenda of the U.S., African and European countries. Over half the women interviewed had spent years in the United States and occasionally in Europe in study or exile. Many had children and other relatives and close friends in diaspora communities – ties that could be exercised for peace. The diaspora networked with groups and individuals having Liberian links and sympathies, collaborated in arranging public meetings, and lobbied politicians and public figures in attempts to maintain external pressure for a solution to the conflict. Friends of Liberia (FOL), Liberian organizations and friends of Liberia in the U.S. and in Europe organized seminars and public meetings to galvanize politicians in those countries to take a more active interest in reaching a peace settlement. Such groups also arranged humanitarian assistance to communities in Liberia and to refugee Liberians in other countries.

Many Liberian women found themselves forced to flee and live as refugees in neighboring countries, as well as in the U.S. and Europe. They often established peace-building and humanitarian activities within their refugee communities and brought relief to those left behind in Liberia. In Ghana, the Côte d'Ivoire and Guinea, they set up groups to deal with community divisions arising in refugee camps, and assigned women to deal with conflict situations as they arose. Those fortunate enough not to be living in camps organized emergency relief for refugee camps in West Africa. Sierra Leonean women living on the border provided shelter, clothing and emotional support to Liberian women and children refugees. They also facilitated travel for Liberian women to the Sierra Leonean capital, Freetown, to participate in peace talks. One woman regularly opened her home to Liberian women for strategic planning sessions on peace and the roles of women in achieving it.

Many of the Liberians interviewed spoke of the importance of meeting women from other conflict areas, such as Bosnia, Rwanda and Uganda. Tonia Wiles remembers a Ugandan woman, met at a London conference, who urged her, "Do not be afraid. Just keep on talking.... Dialogue is a very important process.... At some point in time somebody realizes that what you are saying makes sense, and there is a turn-around."

As they widened their networks, they gained inspiration and training in peace-building at conflict resolution and reconciliation workshops and other programs they attended in Liberia and other African countries such as Zimbabwe and the Côte d'Ivoire, the U.S., England and Sweden. The women mentioned their encounters with International Alert, the Institute for Multi-Track Democracy, the Carter Center and the Nairobi Peace Initiative led by Hezikiah Assafas. Elizabeth Mulbah and Marian Subah attended courses in reconciliation and trauma healing at Eastern Mennonite University in Virginia and developed workshops that were sustained for many years by the Christian Health Association of Liberia. Adama Jawandoh spoke of the "pyramid method of settling disputes from the bottom up," which she learned about in a workshop in Sweden. Deroe Weeks, accompanied by several Liberian children affected by the war, attended a consultation on "The Impact of Armed Conflict on Children" in Côte d'Ivoire. She was inspired by the experience and by the organizer, Graça Machel, Nelson Mandela's wife and the widow of Mozambique's first President, Samora Machel. "When you see these other people, the efforts they make to bring about peace to ensure that we don't do the same things all over the world again, okay, it makes you want to do something yourself."

Elizabeth Mulbah, Executive Director, Christian Health Association of Liberia.

Photo courtesy of U.S. Institute of Peace

As women seized opportunities for links with the Africa regional and global women's movements, their unity grew even as they prepared for international conferences. Miatta Fahnbulleh, the internationally known Liberian singer, sang for peace in performances and on tapes and CDs. Women in exile lobbied government officials in their countries of exile, promoted Liberian peace issues in the media and attempted to ensure good flows of information.

To take their cause even further into the international community, a large group attended the Beijing Fourth World Conference on Women in 1995 and its earlier African Preparatory Conference in Dakar, Senegal, in November 1994.[6] They publicized their struggles and made important connections with women from other countries.

But despite all these diaspora activities, there was still a sense of isolation on the part of many peace activists. Mary Brownell describes an occasion at an international conference in South Africa:

> I became very emotional...we were meeting African women. Each time we met we were talking peace, and they had not identified with us. I told them "We didn't expect for you to take guns and come and fight our battle. But at least for us to hear on the BBC or for us to get some letters of encouragement to say 'We the African women are with you, we identify with you.' I said this will mean more to us than for us African women to just be traveling around, discussing peace, discussing peace, discussing peace. And I think that brought the message home because in no time after that we had a team composed of African women going around to different African countries, especially when there was conflict, trying to give their support to the women.

The turning point for peace: a unified voice of women

There came a time when women decided that relief work and advocacy alone were not enough. They moved to direct political activism. Together, they took to the streets in protest and would soon invade the men's peace talks. When their separate women's organizations came together and formed a united movement for peace, a higher level of impact and respect was accorded their work. That potential for more effective action was the major impetus to develop collaborative action with other civil society groups.

---

[6] See the report presented at both the Dakar and Beijing United Nations world conferences, *Liberia: a Country Report on the Status of Women*, May 5, 1994, written by Vera Gibson of the Ministry of Planning.

Asked why concerted action had not come earlier, Etweda Cooper explains:

> The Federation of Liberian Women's Organizations, an umbrella
> for women's groups, was banned in the 1980s as being political.
> With that banning...the vehicle through which women's voices
> could be heard in unison no longer existed, and women's issues
> were placed on the back burner.[7]

Unified actions came through the new Liberian Women's Initiative (LWI) that
was a movement rather than simply an organization or a coalition of organizations. Mary Brownell describes the formation of LWI as a major turning
point that brought about a stronger and more inclusive peace movement:

> You know, when you look at the frustrating things at that time, the
> women and children were actually the victims of this civil crisis in
> Liberia. I saw other women's groups engaged in
> relief activities, taking food and clothes to dis-
> placed people. But I said that we the women
> should do a little more than that because there
> were still atrocities all around.... And so, this wild
> thought came to me that instead of sitting down
> and saying the men should play the major role [in
> the political peace process], we women should do
> something also, because they were the ones who
> brought about the war. Even though we are the
> weaker sex, [with] voices joined together as one
> we could make an impact on the Liberian society
> and international community.... So we called a
> mass meeting on February 2, 1994, for women
> from all walks of life, regardless of where they
> came from, their ethnic background or religious
> affiliation. And so all these women came to the City Hall...to form
> this pressure group or this movement, to help in the peace process.
> We did not have guns, but we felt that we the women...needed to
> do something.[8]

**Mary Brownell, President,
Liberian Women's Initiative.**

Through the collaboration that formed the LWI, women's groups were able to
consult widely with all sectors and elements of the female population, focus
their demands for disarmament and resolution of the conflict, gain credibility
through the involvement of women in all walks of life and attract attention to
the work they had been doing to bring peace, healing and reconciliation to the
country.

---

[7] The Federation was revived in 1994.

[8] There were three meetings, the first on February 2nd, to organize the group, the second on
February 4th, to finalize a draft position statement for the group, and the third on February
9th, to read and plan circulation of the paper.

Jointly with the Inter-Faith Mediation Council (IFMC) and other civic groups, including the Council of Chiefs and the Justice and Peace Commission of the Catholic Church, women's groups organized the "stay-home" days in March 1995 and early 1996 that followed one organized by Concerned Women of Liberia in 1993. The stay-home days paralyzed Monrovia, closing markets, government buildings, transport and businesses, and were so successful they were called "the ghost town action." These special days gave important impetus to the actions being supported to advance negotiations. Moreover, they helped develop solidarity among the collaborating groups.

Women's organizations also picketed various locations at different times, including the U.S. Embassy, government offices, faction headquarters, UN offices and the embassies of ECOWAS countries. A number of position statements they produced jointly on the conflict and the effects of violence on civilian populations were used to inform relevant international actors about their concerns and to pressure ECOWAS and the UN into more effective, urgent action in assisting the country to resolve the worsening conflict. Individual letters and information were sent to the wives of all of the heads of state in ECOWAS to encourage informal and secondary advocacy – to influence "the nearest head on the pillow."

Liberian women sing and chant in front of the U.S. Embassy.

LWI tried to widen and strengthen the movement by engaging women across the fighting lines through individual personal contacts, but such courageous efforts were dangerous and are not known to have succeeded. Etweda Cooper tells of meeting 25 young fighters – none more than 12 years old – who threatened a group of women from the Liberian Women's Initiative who were attempting to cross the Po River to meet with other women at Bomi in 1994. Mary Brownell adds:

> We were threatened that if we were going to cross the bridge we were going to be shot at…. We had to turn our tails and come back to Monrovia. We were quite disappointed, but in Monrovia we lobbied, protested and were on the streets. Not women alone – men helped too.

AP/Wide World Photo: Schalk van Zuydam

Disarmament first

A key focus of the unified advocacy was disarmament. Women's organizations were active participants in the Civic Disarmament Campaign, chaired
by the Inter-Faith Mediation Council, that organized to promote disarmament
and stop the sales of guns to Liberia. Ruth Sando Perry, former head of the
Liberia Council of State, explains:

> We all know that African countries do not make guns. We don't
> make warlike materials – they're given to us. We take over rich
> resources – gold, diamonds – we sell them and...instead of getting
> things to build our country...[we get things] to destroy our country.
> There were times we told friendly countries: Don't help us kill our-
> selves. Help us bring peace to our country. Stop passing arms
> through our borders. It worked a bit... because for some time the
> Ivorian government stopped the movement of arms across their
> borders. Guinea did the same thing. These are strategies we used.
> We didn't just sit here and talk. We went out, and when the oppor-
> tunity came we spoke about it. We asked for it.

The Cotonou Accord of July 1993 had established terms for a new Liberian
national transitional government (LNTG) that would involve the factions, and
the "voices of the unarmed" were to be represented and a disarmament
process put in place. When these terms were not met, the newly formed LWI
decided to campaign against installation of the transitional government until
the factions were disarmed. An LWI delegation met with the U.S. and Nigerian Ambassadors to Liberia, the OAU representative to Liberia, the Special
Representative of the Secretary-General of the United Nations (UNSRSG)
and the Field Commander of ECOMOG. The delegation expressed opposition
to the installation of the new government before the conditions outlined in the
agreement had been met – especially disarmament – and urged the international representatives at the meeting to ensure that these conditions would be
adhered to.

To increase the pressure for change, LWI sent faxes outlining members' concerns and suggested actions to rectify the situation to the news media and
political actors throughout Africa and the rest of the world. In addition, an
LWI representative was part of a delegation that met with the incoming
ECOWAS Chairman, President Jerry Rawlings of Ghana. They outlined the
risks to community peace processes and the chances for stability in Liberia if
the transitional government were installed without effective disarmament in
place. But the women's concerns were dismissed, and they were told by
Rawlings, "This is the risk we will have to take."

Women take to the streets: peace now and peace forever

Undaunted, LWI organized a public demonstration on March 4, 1994, the day of its formal founding. The Liberian National Transitional Government was installed on March 7th, before disarmament had started and before the non-combatants were included in the government. Outgoing head of the interim government, Amos Sawyer, comments:

> I recall, even up to the day that the interim government was hand-ing over, there were women carrying placards and saying, "Disar-mament has not taken place and this indeed is a mistake." If disar-mament had taken place back in 1994, as indeed it should have, we probably wouldn't have had April 6, 1996 [when the war came to Monrovia]. The advice of women had been "Stick to your agree-ments. Implement your agreements."

One well-attended march was held in response to the women's perception that the first UN Special Representative to Liberia was abetting the militarization of politics by facilitating the handover of power from the interim government to the transitional government before disarmament was started. LWI wrote an open letter to the UN Special Representative on March 17th and held a large march for disarmament on the 26th.

Despite the setback to their advocacy actions, the disarmament campaign continued, gaining momentum as violence followed the installation of the transitional government and as it became increasingly clear that the Cotonou Accord had failed. On a very practical level, some women formed a group, "Funds for Disarmament," with other organizations and individuals. They attempted to buy guns from fighters and then destroy those arms. ECOMOG opposition to this pilot program halted the activity despite the collection of substantial funds with which to start it. But women continued to campaign for full and effective disarmament until the national elections in 1997, protesting the militarization of Liberian politics and social life.

Although numerous demonstrations were organized by LWI, the Women's Development Association of Liberia (WODAL) and other women's organiza-tions on a range of issues, all were based on the shared demand for peace, dis-armament and good governance. Ruth Perry remembers:

> We had peaceful marches, and all women were involved. We had Christian women, we had Muslim women, we had rural women, and we had women from all over who were involved in these peaceful marches to see to it that we were heard one way or the other. We wanted peace now and peace forever in Liberia.

"We are going to use our pens and brains to fight this war and we shall not relent until peace comes to Liberia once more," Mary Brownell remembers saying. One example of women's innovative efforts was LWI's Position Statement on the Resolution of the Four Disputed Ministries that appeared in the press April 7, 1994:

> At present, NPFL has five (5) ministries, ULIMO five (5) and IGNU four (4). Why then, cannot that armless majority, we, the civilians who have no ties or loyalty to any one of the warring factions, recommend outstanding and capable Liberians to be considered by the Council of State for the four disputed ministries?

Thus LWI called for civil society representatives to head the disputed ministries of Defense, Finance, Justice and Foreign Affairs, and they listed the names of several qualified civilians for each ministry.

Also in mid-1994, women's groups including NAWOCOL, Women in Action for Goodwill, Concerned Women of Liberia, LWI and the Federation of Liberian Women joined hands in calling for a Liberian national conference of "the unarmed people of Liberia who are not willing to be mere spectators while armed factions meet to solve the problem they have created."

Women's actions were not limited to marches, petitions and advocacy. Their unity was enhanced by prayer meetings held weekly in churches and mosques throughout the country, and some women's groups organized fasts for peace. Ellen Johnson-Sirleaf recalls:

> When the tensions built in the society to a point when it could cause disruption, women called for prayers or they called for a time of fasting that was a safety valve because it took the heat off. It enabled people to calm down, to go and seek solace.

Members of the Women in Peace Building Network of Liberia pray for peace on an open piece of ground in the James Springs area of Monrovia.

LWI's report of May 20, 1994 contained a section called "Obligatory" which read, "It is binding upon all members of LWI to hold nightly prayer service at 10 o'clock at their respective homes, for the restoration of peace. Other Liberian women and friends of Liberia are encouraged to be part of this exercise." They placed an ad in the newspaper, which said:

> Join the LWI 10 pm Nightly Prayer Chain and Pray
> For the Nation Wherever You May Find Yourself.

AP/WWP/EPA Photo: Kim Ludbrook

As they used all these approaches, the creation of space for dialogue between warring factions and divided communities gained a new urgency, evidenced by the personal risks women took to establish lines of communication between rival factions, transitional governments, ECOWAS, ECOMOG and other actors they felt could hasten an end to the conflict. "We continued using all the strategies we could think about to make our voices heard. We demonstrated on the streets of Monrovia," Mary Brownell says, adding:

> We visited almost all the African countries wherever there was a peace conference going on. There was a time when we even carried letters and hand delivered them to the different warlords, appealing to them as their mothers and sisters to stop this fighting now. We wrote the warlords asking for conferences with them and we met with them.

Etweda Cooper adds:

> We tried everything. We lobbied, picketed, sent faxes, went to conferences without being invited until eventually we were invited.... We published statements in the newspapers...whatever it took to bring peace to the attention of the Liberian people, we did. And I will say that there is a time for each method. There is a time to lobby, there is time to stand your ground, there is a time to give in.... It's just that you have to know when.

WOMEN AT THE PEACE TABLES

From the very beginning of the war, individual Liberian women were actively calling for peace in public meetings both within and outside the country. Ellen Johnson-Sirleaf recalls:

> One of the things that women did...was to decide that foreign countries were not going to dictate totally on their own the political agenda for Liberia. Hence they interposed themselves in the process, took a role, found a seat and were able to influence some of the outcomes.

Early attendance at conferences

Women attended the first major peace meeting in Banjul in August 1990 where an interim government was developed and later established in Monrovia. Several women with strong political affiliations managed to attend peace negotiations on a number of occasions as members of factional delegations and not as representatives of Liberian women. At times considerable tension was engendered by these potentially conflicting positions women occupied, particularly in view of the desire of women's organizations to be seen and treated as politically neutral in their pursuit of peace. The situation was exacerbated by the fact that even those women attending conferences as parts of factional delegations were very few in number.

Some of the earliest involvement of women at the peace tables stemmed from personal access, not necessarily through factional affiliations. For example, working with a small group of men, Victoria Reffell, a journalist and chair of the National Reconciliation and Reunification Commission, was prominent in the organization of the ultimately unsuccessful peace conference in Freetown, Sierra Leone, in 1990. As part of the ad hoc peace initiative promoting those talks, she was in a position to meet with various political representatives, watch the proceedings and identify weaknesses that contributed to the failure of that particular effort. Weade Kobbah Wureh also attended a number of early peace talks when she was Director General of the Liberia Broadcasting System. She saw arrogance and lack of concern for the plight of people and began to question the value of such meetings.

Journalist Victoria Reffell (left), chair of the National Reconciliation and Reunification Commission, with Ruth Sando Perry, head of the 1996-97 transitional government.

Two women, Myrtle Gibson and Muna Wreh, attended the ECOWAS conference in Lomé, Togo, in February 1991 on their own and circulated a paper about how women and children were suffering from the war. Counselor Tiawan Gongloe, who was present at the meeting, remembers:

> They presented a very passionate story and stated that it was necessary for the West African [leaders] to stop the war in Liberia because it was affecting families and that women were pillars of the family and they were feeling the brunt of the war.

As the warring groups proliferated and the war expanded, formal regional peace conferences and initiatives increased. Yet throughout 1991-1993 women's organizations were not recognized as observers or as participants by ECOWAS or by the United Nations. There was an almost universal understanding among women that they and children were disproportionately affected by the conflict and therefore there was an urgent need for them to be active in pursuing peace. As women they had suffered the brutality of the actions of military and warring factions and they had a clear view of the impacts of the conflict on the social, economic and emotional lives of communities. They

Photo courtesy of Musue Haddad

had watched successive ceasefire and peace accords be negotiated (and fail) without acknowledgement of human suffering. It was time to formulate a consolidated view on the conflict and strategies for an effective peace.

Uninvited delegations gain legitimacy

The first attempt that women's organizations made to participate in official peace negotiations was at the Accra Clarification Conference in December 1994. Determined to send a delegation to the conference, even though they had not been invited, the women raised funds from several different sources, relying on personal relationships and the goodwill of organizations and individuals. Having written to ECOWAS for invitations that were not forthcoming, the women made their own way to Accra. Massa Washington, a journalist and humanitarian worker, describes the process:

> We had written to ECOWAS…that the women of Liberia wanted to be represented at this conference and, again, they didn't take us seriously. They thought we were joking, so we proceeded to invite ourselves. We lobbied for tickets and then at the end of the day, we got tickets for six women. But interestingly, most of our benefactors were men…in the private sector, men from civil society.

On their arrival in Accra, the women's delegation was told they could not take part in the conference, so they sat outside the conference hall all day, waiting for breaks in the proceedings, at which point they would lobby faction leaders, international actors, ECOWAS and intergovernmental representatives. While the women were lobbying people directly involved in the peace proceedings, Massa Washington contacted Liberian friends in Ghana, Ghanaian media colleagues and some of the international press attending the conference. She publicized the non-participation of women at the conference and the current dire situation for women and children in Liberia.

The delegation's exclusion from the conference became widely known through Ghanaian and international television, radio and newspaper coverage. As a result of this pressure and the delegation's successful lobbying activities, they were granted official observer status on the second day of the conference. Although unable to actively participate in the proceedings, they were allowed to sit in the conference room, hear the negotiations, analyze the positions of the different actors and identify possibilities for advocacy and mediation. During breaks in the proceedings they continued to lobby and promote their viewpoints on achieving peace. By the third day they received official participant status.

Learning from their participation in the Accra meeting, they realized that to be taken seriously at future meetings they must be armed with written documentation, so a coalition of women's organizations, led by the Liberian Women's Initiative and joined by individual peace activists, organized consultative and drafting meetings with women in all walks of life. The Minister of Planning, Amelia Ward, encouraged this initiative, and her special assistant, Ruth Caesar, played a leading role in sessions at the Ministry of Planning and in the follow-up.

Ruth Caesar was one of the many peace activists who worked ceaselessly behind the scenes to ensure women's participation at the political peace processes:

> [Women] were not placed on government delegations.... I personally never had the opportunity to go to these conferences because we were the ones on the ground moving things...but one thing we were involved in [was] formulating the resolutions, the statements, the papers that were presented to ECOWAS leaders. The women would come here, and we would look at [the documents] and make sure that things [were] all right, that the resources were available, that the meetings were held, you know, like an engine that moves a car.... We all put our hands together.

The women – "hundreds of women" says Theresa Leigh-Sherman – produced a position statement on the conduct of the conflict and its impact on women, children and communities. Using the statement as a mandate, the organizations worked to gain access to the political peace tables and negotiations conducted through ECOWAS, the Organization of African Unity (OAU) and the UN. Leigh-Sherman explains:

> It was a serious paper because we [produced documented facts]. If we said the factions bombed a mosque in Cape Mount, we gave the date and time. If we said a child was raped, we gave the place. It was not a passionate thing, it was a factual paper.

Although buoyed by the production of a mandate, the women had no resources to attend the peace negotiations, which were regularly held outside of Liberia. Several women's groups undertook fundraising activities in Liberia to support sending a delegation to the ECOWAS Heads of State Mediation Committee in Abuja, Nigeria, in May 1995. Once again, women had not been invited to take part. They elected two women to go, Theresa Leigh-Sherman and Evelyn Townsend, and Clara d'Almeida joined the team. Leigh-Sherman, an entrepreneur and educator, recalls the difficulties:

> Of course we were not on the agenda, but we got to Abuja.... We were so bad off financially, we hardly had clothes, I mean we had nothing except will power. We were proud to be Liberians, and we

felt it was time for the international community to hear our side of the story. So we...asked friends and we took collections, and that's how we bought our tickets.

The right to be seen, to be heard, to be counted

Once they arrived in Abuja, the three-woman delegation began lobbying for an opportunity to present their position paper to the meeting on behalf of the women of Liberia. Contacts in Nigeria were mobilized to meet decision makers and to advocate on behalf of the delegation. Individual meetings were held with separate heads of state to whom they had access as well as international representatives and ECOWAS officials. Some leaders listened keenly and sympathetically, but usually responses were, "The program is set; you're not on the agenda," or "It's never been done before." Then, at the opening meeting, President Jerry Rawlings presented the women with an opportunity to participate. Theresa Leigh-Sherman will remember that moment for the rest of her life:

Educator Theresa Leigh-Sherman.

He said, "Now ladies and gentlemen we're going to deviate for the first time in ECOWAS. We have listened to the men, we have listened to all the factions...but we have never listened to the civilians, we have never listened to our mothers, we have never listened to our sisters. We have a delegation of Liberian women and they want us to hear what they have to say, and we feel as a community it is only fair." We just grabbed each other's hands, we were shaking because it looked [like] God had heard our prayers. I just took that...paper...and slowly we talked about the killing and how these men were opening these women's stomachs and betting on the babies. We talked about everything because the women were tired. We were just tired. It was a 30-minute paper. We made recommendations. And I tell you the nine Presidents that were there and...CNN, BBC, everybody was in tears because these are facts that these people didn't know about.... But we had gone through it. We had lost everything we worked for.

Theresa Leigh-Sherman's presentation included a number of recommendations on the process of disarmament and a government of inclusion. One key recommendation, number 5, concerned the participation of women:

We hereby reiterate our demand that the women of Liberia be included in all discussions on matters concerning the state and the welfare

> of the people. Our lack of representation in the ongoing peace process is equivalent to the denial of one of our fundamental rights: the right to be seen, be heard, and be counted. This [denial] also deprives the country [of] access to the opinion of 51 percent of its human resources in solving the problems, which affect our lives as a people.

This statement shocked ECOWAS members as it referred to the "bandits" and pressed the women's position of "no elections without disarmament." News reports commended this unprecedented presentation. Liberian women as a group had made their presence felt at the negotiating tables and, although they would continue to struggle for full representation, they had established a precedent for participation in the search for peace.

When your mother calls you, you must show up

Recognition at Abuja was followed by a major achievement in peacemaking and mediation by women's organizations. "After the May meeting, ECOWAS encouraged women to find ways to get the leaders to talk to each other," Ruth Caesar recalls. Evelyn Townsend remembers how the women received word that "the factions are still at each other's throats.... We give you a week, if you can call the factions together." This signal led to their major mediation effort with all faction leaders, supported by the United Nations. It took place at the National Bank Conference Room in Monrovia in July of 1995. Many Liberians see it as a key turning point in the long-running peace process.

The focus of the meeting was straightforward: to bring representatives of the various warring factions to Monrovia for a joint meeting and to provide a space for interaction and dialogue. The factions would discuss their understandings of the conflict and the issues it raised and then begin to consider how it might be resolved.

Analysis of the mediation at the National Bank centers on the meeting itself, but it is clear that the mediation never would have taken place if not for a series of individual meetings between women and different faction leaders prior to the meeting. As part of their general advocacy work, women's organizations had formed delegations from varying backgrounds (rural, urban, professional, farmers, marketers etc.) to visit the homes or headquarters of all faction leaders in order to establish communication links. This laid the foundation of trust, goodwill and a perceived neutrality, which women at a later date were able to harness to promote the mediation meeting. The method used reflected some traditional Liberian conflict resolution techniques: hold individual meetings with the participants of the conflict and then bring them together for a joint meeting to resolve differences. Senator Evelyn Townsend explains:

The thing is to make them comfortable. The other thing is not to be biased. You accept everybody on the same level and don't start your guilt trip on anybody. When they find out you're objective they will open up to you, and that was our experience – they did open up to us all the time. We were able to go where many people dared not go because they had a lot of confidence [in us]. We built confidence before we started talking to them. And so they believed us when we talked.

Elizabeth Mulbah, director of the Christian Health Association of Liberia, and her CHAL colleague, Marian Subah, agreed to facilitate the session. They themselves were not prominent in the political life of Liberia, and they were not members of the women's groups. There were two other peace meetings on the same day – one sponsored by the Inter-Faith Mediation Council and another by the political parties, but the leaders of the different factions agreed to have strong representation at the meeting being sponsored by the women's organizations. The women made daily contacts with the leaders in advance to assure their attendance, found a safe venue at the National Bank, got ECO-MOG security, and assured the factions that there would be no press coverage. They made certain that the factions agreed to the choice of facilitators, and they all observed a day of fasting and prayer before the meeting took place.

> I've worked with a lot of women in peace efforts, and a lot of men supported us – donated materials, time, money. But men were more prone to say, "Let's go flush them out. Let's go kill them." Women would say, "Let's go talk to the boys."
>
> *Etweda Cooper*
> *Secretary General, LWI*

The meeting began three hours late, but all factions were represented and four persons ("four of their best") were present from each. "When your mother calls you, you must show up," said one. The facilitators began with prayers, then the group set up basic guidelines for the session. One day grew into four days. Each day the facilitators did a variety of exercises that encouraged cooperation and different styles of behavior. Mulbah and Subah stressed that there were no ready-made answers and that the outcomes depended on those who were present – not the facilitators or the observers from the women's organizations. The participating faction leaders discussed such problems as how to decide who should lead what ministries in a coalition government and how to convince opposing leaders that these might be good choices. The facilitators used newsprint for recording the highlights of the discussions.

Women from organizations sponsoring the event observed the sessions. They did not take part, but they did carefully intercede with individual faction representatives if they became angry and sought to leave. One described such a conversation:

My man where are you going?" I asked. "That man said something," he replied. "Never mind. Just come back because this is
Liberia we are talking about. It is greater than all of you."

Clara d'Almeida describes her experience at the meeting:

> Elizabeth Mulbah did some sort of reconciliation thing, starting
> from scratch, as if they were all children again. It was a beautiful
> program. Every day when we got there, it was…saying your
> prayers and meditating on what had transpired, and she'd go
> through this whole thing. She was talking to them, reading to them,
> playing different games with them. At one time she had pieces of
> paper which [they] wrote on and turned face down. Everybody was
> supposed to pick one with somebody's name and say something
> nice to that person. Can you imagine these people who had been
> fighting each other all along and all of a sudden have to tell each
> other something nice? When we first got in there it was as if every-
> body was ready for a fight. Gradually we saw them simmering
> down. By the time the conference was over, people were able to
> stand up and pat each other on the back…. And at the end of the
> meeting they softened the position that they were all holding…. To
> me that was the breaking point of what we have today.

Other outside commentators had similar feelings. In the words of Conmany
Wesseh of the Center for Democratic Empowerment (CEDE):

> The meeting at the National Bank was ice-breaking…was very crit-
> ical. It came at a time when things seemed to have broken down,
> when there was serious fatigue on the side of everybody…. I think
> it created a certain kind of opening, which at that point appeared to
> have been closed.

The facilitators later learned that some of the techniques they had used were
introduced at other peace meetings where faction representatives recommended that they use the approach adopted at the National Bank sessions.

A glimmer of peace at last: Abuja I and Abuja II

Despite their recognition at the May 1995 Abuja meeting and the success of
the National Bank session, women still were not accorded a place at the crucial meeting at Abuja in July 1995. However, the outcome of the meeting was
in line with some of the hopes that women had expressed at the time – that
faction leaders come to Monrovia to live. The women hoped that in this way
the factions would be more controlled. Unfortunately, this did not happen. In
April 1996, terrible fighting broke out in Monrovia, and peace did not return
to the city until June.

In August 1996, an invitation was extended to a women's delegation to attend another Abuja peace conference that month. At the conference, to her surprise and that of others, Ruth Sando Perry, a member of the delegation led by Chief Tamba Taylor and an active member of women's peace organizations for several years, was nominated and selected as Head of the Council of State that would oversee the Liberian elections of 1997 and hand over governmental authority to the elected government. Her attendance at the meeting reflected women's continuing challenges in taking part in the peace process:

> I went to Abuja…and when I got there I was told my name was not on the list so I could not be accredited. When I went downstairs, I met the Chief of Protocol, and I told him that I had been refused accreditation and he told me there was nothing that he could do. Fortunately, when he said there was nothing he could do, some boys came and surrounded him and told him, "The Papay [big man] say you should take us for accreditation." So I followed, and when they got their accreditation, [the Chief of Protocol] was embarrassed. He told the man [at the accreditation table], "Look, you have to let this woman have her card," but the man said no…and quarrelled with him. And he told the man, "Look, this is a Senator." I said, "No, former Senator," and he said, "Madam, once a Senator, always a Senator." I said, "Thank you" and kept quiet. In the process he gave me a paper and took my picture, and I was accredited.

Ruth Sando Perry being sworn in as head of Liberia's third transitional government.

The appointment of Ruth Perry to head the transitional government was a great achievement for Liberian women peace activists and one that Mrs. Perry acknowledged.

> I felt the strength, the need, the will power to take it and move on. But not alone – I decided to first of all put it to prayer. Then, secondly, I mobilized the women and challenged them because I felt this challenge was not for Ruth Perry alone. It was for the women of Liberia and African women as a whole.

The day after the election a number of women present at Abuja II, including women of different delegations and Liberian women residing in the U.S., went to her to celebrate and offer their support.

Ellen Johnson-Sirleaf recalls the way in which Ruth Perry successfully maintained the fragile peace and led Liberia to democratic elections in 1997: "Women represented us well. She [Ruth Perry] dispelled the myth that women cannot be leaders."

Annie Saydee, Rural Women's Association president, speaks of other achievements:

> Even though we were going all over to talk to people in the various counties, this southeastern part of the country was not included. Those four counties were out, and they never received food from anywhere because they say the road was blocked. So nobody traveled there until Ruth Perry got there.... She [found] a way for southeastern people to get something to eat.

Others speak of other qualities, including her strength in managing a difficult process, her excellent conflict management skills, her success in enabling a peaceful transition period and her integrity in standing down gracefully at the end of her term.

Ruth Perry herself states:

> To a large extent I succeeded because I had a well-defined goal and objectives in mind. I remained very focused on the mandate given me and did not lobby to become any more influential than being an advocate for peace. My position was clear: I wanted unconditional peace for Liberia.... I projected myself as a true mother and a stabilizer, using faith, discipline, courage, patience and tolerance. Prior to becoming head of state, I was deeply involved in encouraging and motivating women and all patriotic Liberians to take an active part in the peace process.

Before the elections, those organizations that had built good community-based programs such as LWI, promoted equal participation of women through voter education outreach activities and urged women to take part in the post-conflict peace process. Others operated as observers of the election process itself, to ensure that it was peaceful and fully participatory.

The designation of modern Africa's first woman head of state was extremely important and celebrated as such. After their huge efforts, Liberian women felt rewarded by the appointment of Ruth Perry. However, they were aware that the election of one woman to a position of authority, particularly when surrounded by men with varying political motivations, could not guarantee the achievement of Liberian women's hopes for peace and reconciliation.

SETBACKS, SUCCESSES AND CHALLENGES

Elizabeth Mulbah encapsulates the women's view of the setbacks they experienced: "It was not always a success story, but I think lives have been touched." In considering the challenges and setbacks it is important to remember the chronically difficult, insecure, violent and unsupported context in which women worked for peace. While lessons will assist in strengthening future work, the fact that so many initiatives were successfully undertaken under such stressful circumstances cannot be overemphasized.

> What actually got me involved was when I saw my childhood friend shy away from me because I was living in Monrovia and they were living in Gbarnga "behind the lines." We've known each other since we were in diapers. We were not enemies yet we could not communicate because we lived on opposite sides of the divide. That made me realize how foolish we all were. We all were bleeding for our country yet we felt we were at such odds, and it was not true. There was nothing dividing us other than this imaginary line of support for one person or the other.
>
> *Etweda Cooper, Secretary General, LWI*

There were indeed some outstandingly successful peace initiatives by women during the conflict. Not all of them had the hoped-for results, however, and, in addition, collaboration among women's organizations proved at times difficult to achieve or maintain. Differing political, religious, social and economic affiliations made women vulnerable to splits within their organizations and among themselves. To make the situation even more complex, women lived with high levels of personal insecurity caused by the conflict and heightened by the risks they took in order to continue their work for peace. Yet the sense of danger and risk with which they lived throughout the conflict often became a unifying factor for them. "We were determined to do this no matter what would be the consequences," Mary Brownell says.

Every imaginable obstacle stood in the way of success. Continuing violence, with regular instances of displacement and relocation, often disrupted advocacy and mediation efforts during the initial, seven-year conflict. Initiatives that involved travel were halted due to difficulties of passing through areas controlled by warring factions, and initiatives involving material assistance were hampered by the lack of access to resources.

During periods of violence in Monrovia, for example, peace activities were constantly disrupted. Offices and homes where women leaders worked or lived were often vandalized, and many were forced to flee the country. At times, fear that a particular woman's activities would attract adverse attention to her community or groups to which she was affiliated meant that she would be isolated or pressured to curtail her actions. When women began to organize more effectively, such pressures intensified and they were subjected to personal and public verbal assaults on their integrity and motivation. Massa

Washington recalls one man who viewed LWI members as "frustrated women whose husbands had left them."

It must be understood that not all women acted for peace. Conmany Wesseh says:

> Let's make it clear: it is not that all women had exactly the same position. There were some women who worked with faction leaders, who supported the war or who worked in ways that contributed to and supported the war. There were women who were fighters.

And some who belonged to women's organizations working for peace continued to maintain political/factional allegiances. This type of dual membership could cause tension among women peace activists, occasionally making them vulnerable to accusations of partiality, particularly when such allegiances had not been openly declared. Women's organizations wanted to be seen as strictly impartial. There are stories of women who were judged to be betraying the movement by giving information to groups with which they were politically affiliated or making information public. One activist recalls:

> What was surprising was that whenever we met and planned a strategy, by evening it was all over the radio station.

On the other hand, there were advantages to dual allegiances. The faction members were able to present to their faction leaders the concerns of large numbers of women about the conflict being waged against the civilian population. They became peace advocates within their factions. But dual memberships – in women's peace groups and in warring factions – could be looked at with suspicion by factions who saw the peace activities of their women members as avenues for potential disloyalty.

Occasionally, internal rivalries among women's groups blocked progress in other activities, as at the second Liberian National Conference in late 1994 when women failed to unite to nominate and back one candidate for the position of civilian representative on the Council of State for the transitional government. As a result, the vote for women was split and a man was selected. Women were wiser in 1996 when Ruth Perry was chosen.

STEPS TOWARD LASTING PEACE

By cooperating on a unified strategy, women's groups harnessed the power and commitment of many women who were living, surviving and sustaining life at the front lines of the conflict. This power was evident in the strength and success of many of the peace activities where there was true integration or collaboration with rural women in particular. Mary Brownell pays tribute to the rural women involved in LWI:

> Most of those sisters, even though unlettered, had the vision, and
> they have been instrumental in going out to spear[head] the peace
> process.

The groundwork laid through the myriad activities undertaken by women,
sometimes on their own and sometimes in collaboration with men, cannot and
should not be underestimated. It is crucial also that initiatives undertaken outside of political peace negotiations and processes are not stripped of their
inherently political meanings, outcomes and impacts, making them even more
likely to be disregarded.

Ruth Caesar applauds the way rural women transformed their peace-building
activities into post-conflict support for the electoral process and economic
development:

> These women…are able now, during the time of the elections, to go
> to their counties themselves, to sensitize women to vote. They are
> sufficiently sensitized today that they have established the Rural
> Women's Association…and those women are working now toward
> establishing a banking system for rural women.

Still other organizations with explicit peace-building objectives have established human and women's rights education projects, as Evelyn Kandakai
explains:

> …to maintain…peace [by building] on the democratic process that
> has started, so that it can be well grounded. We need to have mass
> education to support this democratic process and we need to
> advance the gains made by civil society during the war, using peace
> making and using the quest for peace as a rallying point to contin-
> ue to…make a stronger civil society.

The meaning of peace

Women's solidarity was strengthened by their shared understanding of the
meaning of peace, peacemaking and peacekeeping. In the early stages of the
conflict many of them participated in the actions of the Inter-Faith Mediation
Committee – undoubtedly the civil society organization with the highest level
of activity and the greatest impact on peace-building initiatives at the time.
That participation testifies to the fact that religious beliefs, reflected in
extremely high levels of affiliation to churches and mosques, are the foundation of many Liberian women's commitments to peacemaking and their con-
viction that peace must start with the individual. As threats to survival grew

and the need for personal peace intensified, non-traditional spiritual movements became stronger and were often led by powerful women whose fol-
lowers crossed ethnic and class lines. That these leaders were "persons of
God, who can be trusted" was an additional basis for solidarity among
women. Whether undertaking peace initiatives alone or as members of civil
society groups, they believed that families, communities and government
have crucial roles in fostering and sustaining peace in a society.

Women join governments, international agencies and civil society groups in
debating definitions and perceptions of peace and the social and political
agendas attached to them because they are aware that definitions can have
major impacts, not only on understanding and actions that promote or sustain
peace but also on the allocation of resources for such activities. They know
that, if political mediation is seen as the primary method of peace-making, the
importance of other interventions and actions, such as their own to promote
peace will be undervalued. Because they are woefully underrepresented in
most political mediation processes, their other peacemaking activities are in
fact often undervalued, as Deroe Weekes explains:

> I think maybe part of the thing is that people, women, individuals,
> all over, maybe we feel that…if we're not involved in the political
> peace process, we're not doing anything as far as peacemaking is
> concerned.

Yet women know that peacemaking is more than a political process. Dorothy
Musuleng Cooper explains what peace means to her:

> On the personal level, peace for me is…a positive frame of mind –
> psychological well-being that allows me to be able to live from day
> to day as a rational, thinking, caring, responsible person. Peace on
> the national level for me means that we have a stable, elected gov-
> ernment that has the capability to administer the affairs of the coun-
> try, giving consideration to all sectors, all indigenes, all aspects of
> the people and governance. That there are no insurrections, there
> are no military outbreaks. That law and law enforcement will be
> respected and that the people in these areas are of the caliber that
> will command the respect and cooperation of the people. Again,
> peace on the social level means that we realize, all of us, the impor-
> tance of individuals as human beings, and we respect their rights to
> live and operate as independent human beings. That people realize
> our interdependence and the necessity to work together as a people
> in various groups but having a thread of unity running throughout.

Musuleng Cooper illustrates the trend also evident in professional conflict
resolution and peace-building circles to perceive peace-building as a whole
range of actions and activities – from macro-level processes and interven-

tions, such as political mediation and advocacy activities, to those at the micro level, including reconciliation initiatives and human rights education:

> Peace-building is a whole process of restructuring what has been destroyed – harmony, trust and working for a common agenda.[9]

> **Peace to me is when there is no more running. The guns are silent. But the real peace is when you can get up in the morning and be able to find something to eat and not run to get it. Peace is when you can laugh and from the bottom of your heart because you can put food on the table for your children to eat and not sit there and worry.**
>
> *Clara d'Almeida*

In a recent consultation, Liberians in rural areas articulated conceptions of peace that encompassed physical, emotional and spiritual healing, reconstruction of all elements of their society and included issues relating to social justice and the roots of the conflict.[10]

The range of peace-building activities supported by these perceptions necessitates a wide variety of actors – individuals in different communities, government, national and international organizations. Those specializing in peace-building work discard narrow perceptions, which define peace only in relation to war, and highlight the roles of women in family and societal reconciliation in stable as well as less stable political settings. Women peacemakers in Liberia recognize many of the activities described above as peacemaking. They are inspiring, as are their actions to build peace.

Evelyn Townsend remembers:

> We took to the streets, we cried, we begged, we met in groups, we made certain decisions as we [said] that we wouldn't be satisfied until there was peace.

> **Peace certainly for me does not mean solely the absence of war. It means a secure atmosphere to allow people to live, grow and work, and to realize their potentials without any molestation, harassment, intimidation or interference in their lives.**
>
> *Weade Kobbah Wureh*

But peace must be constantly pursued, as Weade Kobbah Wureh understands:

> We've come to where we say we have a semblance of it because of the absence of war, but I think there's a lot to be done in the area of peace-building. Peace can be built and sustained in Liberia by ensuring that those things that threaten individual security, whatever these insecurities are, are removed.

---

[9] Quoted in Nasri A. Adam, IIDA Women's Development Organization, *Best Practices in Peace-Building and Non-Violent Conflict Resolution*, UNHCR, UNESCO, UNDP, UNFPA, UNICEF, UNIFEM, undated.

[10] Philippa Atkinson, *NGOs and Peace-Building in Complex Political Emergencies: A Study of Liberia*, Institute for Development Policy and Management, University of Manchester, UK, June 2000.

These many facets of peacemaking are echoed in the report of the Secretary-General of the United Nations: *The causes of conflict and the promotion of durable peace and sustainable development in Africa.* He includes "negotiation, mediation, good offices, fact-finding missions and judicial resolution" as elements of peacemaking. He adds that "the objectives include facilitating dialogue, defusing tensions, promoting national reconciliation, advancing respect for human rights and institutionalizing peace."[11]

> **For me, peace means economic security. Peace means not just the absence of war or to be able to sleep at night, peace means being able to sustain your family. Peace means being able to do the things that you dream of. It means being able to do the things that will promote your country and your society.**
>
> *Etweda Cooper*

The value of recognition

It is clear that women's hard-won recognition of their delegations at the Accra and Abuja conferences provided a platform for future actions and gave greater recognition and weight to the many other elements of their peacemaking work during the conflict, nationally and internationally, despite the tendency for many people involved in conflict and conflict resolution to emphasize activities focused on the political aspects of the peace process.

By the time of the 1997 elections, women's peace efforts had gained a high degree of credibility and, in later analyses of the Liberian conflict, their conflict resolution and peace-building efforts have at times been given a recognition that was lacking at the time they occurred.

> **Even giving someone a cup of water is peace.... If you sat down with a group of women to discuss their problems, that is peace.... If you shared your meal with another family who came into the displaced camp you were in, that's peace. If you talked to a young girl who was raped, that's peace. So we had to get involved in all those things.**
>
> *Ruth Caesar*

Like other Liberians, women lived in conditions of constant insecurity and both random and organized violence. As their peace activities gained greater recognition and publicity, the risks that they lived with increased. But despite the risks and setbacks, individual women and women's groups continued their peace efforts, encouraged by their successes and determined to learn from their setbacks. They were keenly aware that their activities were part of a long, ongoing process. Failures were to be expected, and successes were to be celebrated, and both were acknowledged as pieces in a very large puzzle, much of which was beyond their control.

---

[11] Annan, Kofi A., *The Causes of Conflict and the Promotion of Durable Peace and Sustainable Development in Africa*, A/52/871, United Nations, 1998.

Hundreds of Liberian women continue their protest at the Executive Mansion in Monrovia urging dialogue between the government and rebels.

Part II:
THE CONTINUING STRUGGLE FOR PEACE AND GENDER JUSTICE

> Peace accords are often seen as a culminating point of a peace process. In the language of governments and the military the accords are referred to as an end-game scenario.... In reality the accords are nothing more than opening a door into a whole new labyrinth of rooms that invite us to continue in the process of redefining our relationships.
>
> *John Paul Lederach, Professor of International Peace-building*
> *University of Notre Dame and Eastern Mennonite University*

The signing of the Abuja peace accords, the 1997 national elections and the establishment of the elected government of President Charles Taylor marked the conclusion of one phase of the Liberian conflict and peace process. Yet the struggle left a bitter inheritance. Liberians had to cope with the ravages of the conflict – even while new battles raged. They mourned the multitudes who had died as more were being killed. They struggled to keep in touch with vast numbers of family and community members who became refugees in other countries and in internally displaced camps. They struggled to rebuild homes and institutions that were destroyed, to comfort the thousands of women and girls who were raped – often when in search of food – and they confronted an economy in disarray.

Liberia's situation is chilling. In September 2002, the *Economist Intelligence Unit Survey* revealed that the infant mortality rate was 147 per 1000 and life expectancy 48 years.[1] In April 2003, Minister of Health Peter Coleman announced that Liberia ranked 174th out of 175 countries in the UNDP Development Index, with 80 percent of the population living below the poverty line and 90 percent of the work force unemployed.

Most troubling of all is the fact that fighters still waged civil war. The exodus of ECOWAS soldiers after the 1997 elections left the country in postwar chaos, with inadequate policing and broken infrastructure. Many soldiers were never disarmed, security forces were never trained and small arms continue to be readily available. None of these factors foster peaceful development. Would this dangerous situation exist if women had been half of the peace negotiation teams, and if the disarmament movement of women and

---

[1] *Economist Intelligence Unit Quarterly Report on Liberia,* September 2002.

men had succeeded in stalling the 1997 elections until disarmament was complete?

Sporadic outbreaks of violence in 1997 and 1998 were followed by sustained fighting between government forces and new factions. Between 2000 and 2003, the fighting between government troops and members of LURD (Liberians United for Reconciliation and Democracy) flowed back and forth across Liberia. Towns such as Zorzor, Bopolu and Gbarnga repeatedly changed hands. The accompanying looting, raping and other human rights violations led refugees to flee toward what they hoped were more secure destinations. In early 2003, a new faction, MODEL (Movement for Democracy in Liberia), launched attacks and gained control of much of the southeast of the country.

A young woman holding her baby stands in the middle of a street in the interior town of Bong Mines. Isolated by the civil conflict, the town supports up to 10,000 displaced persons and continues to be fought over by warring factions.

Meanwhile, chaos affected other countries in the region. The civil war in Sierra Leone ended, but 50,000 Sierra Leonean refugees remained in Liberia, threatened by the continuous fighting. In May 2003, the United Nations reported that more than 200,000 Liberians had fled to neighboring countries to escape the struggles between LURD and Liberian government troops, and 130,000 Liberians were internally displaced.

Around the same time, a civil war in Côte d'Ivoire endangered eastern Liberia. Thousands of Ivorians, Malians, Ghanaians and Sierra Leoneans fled to eastern Liberia to escape the fighting in the Côte d'Ivoire. Liberian refugees in the Côte d'Ivoire were recruited to fight on both sides of that country's civil conflict. It was hoped that a May 2003 ceasefire and confining the fighters to military camps would relieve what the United Nations has described as "a deteriorating humanitarian crisis."

During this difficult period from 1997 to 2003, Liberian women have shown that they are not prepared to go back to "business as usual." They have sought to maintain the roles they had assumed and the skills they had gained in working for peace during wartime. They continued to build on the multidimensional approaches toward peace that they developed individually and collectively during the 1990s.

Women's organizations initiated reconciliation and reconstruction programs, planned and carried out new regional peace initiatives in cooperation with women of Sierra Leone and Guinea, and – encouraged by the international women's movement – sought a peace that included gender justice and equality.

RECONCILIATION AND RECONSTRUCTION INITIATIVES

Following the 1997 peace agreement, many women and women's organizations that had actively pursued peace during the conflict expanded their work and engaged in reconciliation and reconstruction activities that were vitally important after the devastating experiences faced during the war. In 1994 for instance, the World Health Organization reported that nearly two-thirds of high school students in Liberia had seen someone killed, tortured or raped and that 77 percent of these students had lost a close relative. Liberian women peace activists emphasized that this scale of loss and witness to violence leaves individuals and communities with deep scars that must be healed if the country is not to reap a whirlwind of social violence at a later stage.

According to Ruth Sando Perry:

> For seven years we were at war, a senseless war, and we did not realize [any] good out of it except death and destruction.... We have to make sure that reconciliation, genuine reconciliation takes place among us and that we do not only talk about reconciliation just within the proximity of where we live, but [that] we carry it...into every little village, every little town, every little county, to the people in churches, in schools.... What we did within this Paynesville community [and elsewhere] was open the lines of communication [among] us. People spoke out about the ill treatment, the destructive way things happened within their community. They spoke about...the inhumane way people were treated.... So we...decided that it [was] about time we pour out these things. We will not forget, but we must learn to forgive and move on with life. We should start respecting [each other]; we should start having respect for human rights and be law-abiding citizens. We have to start educating and advocating [to] build a society in which we can all live as one big family. Be my keeper and I'll be your keeper – good neighbors. These are some of the things we have been discussing within the neighborhoods.

Mary Brownell reflects on some of the benefits and difficulties of this reconciliation work:

> [The Liberian Women's Initiative initiated a] peace seminar, going to different villages and talking to our people out there – especial-

ly the women – on how we can reconcile with one another even
though it's hard…. And I would say [from the assessment that I
read] that after [visits to] five or six of these centers, [the women]
were very happy that the exercise had brought them together, and
[that] they were able to mingle and work together.

The women who participated in the "Bridges of Peace" initiative helped to
reunite their communities. But, as Mary Brownell observes:

The only [difficulty] I saw was that [the women] had expected
more than just LWI talking to them about compromising, forgiving
and reconciliation. They had hoped that LWI would be in the position to give them some seed money to turn over and do business
themselves…. Nobody can actually say you have peace, peace of
mind, if you are hungry, if you don't have food to eat, you do not
know where the next meal is coming from, how your children will
go to school.

Liberia's economy has been destroyed by continuing armed conflict, and
there has been no economic revitalization. The government has spent more
than 50 percent of its budget on military operations, and donors have limited
their assistance to humanitarian aid.[2] The economic outlook was worsened by
UN Security Council sanctions, initially imposed in 2001 due to strong evidence of the Liberian government's support of rebel groups in Sierra Leone
that are accused of killing, raping and maiming tens of thousands of people.

As a direct consequence of the government's declining revenue, unemployment has escalated, and the majority of the population struggle for survival.
Large arrears of civil-service pay and social services were increasingly provided by humanitarian agencies. In 1998, Elizabeth Sele Mulbah foresaw the
crucial significance of these challenges:

It's disheartening…to work one month and go home with a salary
that cannot buy a bag of rice. It's a crime if somebody is sick and
cannot afford the medical care that they need. It's a crime if children of school age cannot go to school, either because there are no
schools to go to or there are no funds…. It's a crime if a family
cannot feed itself. So if we are going to have peace, genuine peace
that will last, …some basic hierarchy of needs must be met.

Groups of women working in urban and rural communities on conflict resolution and reconciliation have begun to include communal economic development projects, such as constructing a community drainage system, supporting income generation and micro-credit schemes or building a new
school, to promote economic security and reconciliation simultaneously.

---

[2] *Economist Intelligence Unit Quarterly Report on Liberia,* September 2002.

The YWCA is one women's organization that has assisted hundreds of victimized women and children, helping to empower them to move on. For example, one woman, called Elizabeth, had known horror when the rebels decapitated her husband. Now, helped by 11 men and women, she runs an orphanage named Children's Ministry for 30 boys and 15 girls aged 6 months to 16 years. They farm to feed themselves.

Women such as the members of AFELL, the Association of Female Lawyers of Liberia, have successfully introduced significant legislation on child soldiers and gender issues and given legal support to women. For instance, AFELL brought the case of a 24-year-old teacher called McVilla, to the courts. "For the first time a woman rape victim has brought charges and started legal proceedings against her aggressors," Elizabeth Boyemeh explains. McVilla speaks at press conferences, publicly naming her rapists and displaying medical reports.[3]

Meanwhile, Liberian women leaders in the peace movement have strengthened their peace efforts by joining with counterparts in adjacent countries to form a regional peace network.

REGIONAL PEACE INITIATIVES

At the Fifth World Conference on Women at Beijing in 1995, Mary Brownell spoke of the isolation she felt because of the lack of encouragement from other African women. Two years later, during the Liberian elections, a large delegation of women representing Femmes Afrique Solidarité (FAS) was on hand to observe the elections and encourage the women who had worked for peace. Soon after the elections, FAS carried out a training program on advocacy and lobbying techniques towards assisting women's organizations to consolidate the peace process and reconstruct their country. In February 1998, FAS joined UNIFEM, UNHCR, UNDP and the Liberian government on a needs-assessment mission about the activities of women's organizations in communities and refugee camps.

The contact with FAS continued, and solidarity has been built with other women of peace in Africa. Liberian women peace activists in the '90s, including Theresa Leigh-Sherman, Ruth Caesar, Mary Brownell, Elizabeth Mulbah and Evelyn Kandakai, among others, managed to create and encourage regional and international alliances despite difficulties of communication, travel, lack of funding and little encouragement from those in power.

---

[3] Achtelstetter, Karin, "Every one a heroine – the lives of women in Liberia," Common Concern Magazine, September 2000, World YWCA website: www.worldywca.org/common_concern/sept2000/ LibHeroine.html

As conflict became regional, they developed a network among peace activists from Liberia, Sierra Leone and Guinea, countries that form the Mano River Union, a customs union established in 1974 to strengthen the economies of member nations. The Union now concerns itself with other issues, such as fighting HIV/AIDS, despite the serious tensions and divisions that exist among the three countries whose leaders suspect their neighbors of supporting rebel movements within their own boundaries.

A three-day meeting sponsored by the Economic Community for West Africa (ECOWAS) in November 1999 in Abuja, Nigeria, was the occasion for women of Liberia, Sierra Leone and Guinea to express concerns about their shared problems. There they laid the groundwork for a women's peace network. In May 2000, the Mano River Union Women Peace Network (MARWOPNET) was formed by 56 participants from the three countries at a second three-day meeting in Abuja.

Besides determining the structure and purposes of MARWOPNET, participants designed a campaign for a culture of peace in the Mano River Union countries. They urged ECOWAS to help establish a secure environment through monitoring small arms trafficking, addressing disarmament and developing programs for child soldiers, planning programs for those traumatized by war and encouraging women's self reliance through training in entrepreneurial skills. To ensure their long-term concerns for peace, the women

Women from Guinea, Liberia and Sierra Leone – all members of the Mano River Women Peace Network (MARWOPNET) – join forces at a leadership training workshop in Abidjan in June 2001.

Photo courtesy of Elizabeth Mulbah

also proposed that the ECOWAS mechanism for conflict resolution be amended to allow three positions for women at high levels.

MARWOPNET was also active on the ground. In March of 2001, they held two days of peace talks with women refugees at camps in the Kissidougou district of Guinea to express solidarity and to ask for their full involvement in efforts to restore peace. In December of the same year, a delegation of MARWOPNET women was invited to attend the 25th Summit of ECOWAS Heads of state in Dakar, Senegal. The delegation was briefed by Amelia Ward, Liberian Minister of Economic and Social Affairs, and met with media representatives. In their closing communiqué they commented:

> As citizens of the three [Mano River] countries, mothers, spouses and sisters, [we seek] lasting peace, security and stability in the sub-region.[4]

To gain Africa-wide solidarity among women, in April 2001 MARWOPNET participated in a consultation on enhancing women's participation in peace-building sponsored by the UN Economic Commission for Africa and the UN Division for the Advancement of Women together with representatives of 10 war-torn African countries. There, the Liberian representative explained how women in the Mano River region were given audience at all levels, including with heads of state. Their relationship with ECOWAS was praised for its support of women's addressing the highest policy organizations in the sub-region.

The MARWOPNET network continued to grow stronger through training sessions held in June and July 2002, in Abidjan, through encouragement from other African women's groups and through such actions as demonstrations, a silent peace march in Monrovia and regular prayer meetings.

The most significant political actions of MARWOPNET have been their separate meetings with the leaders of Guinea, Liberia and Sierra Leone to convince them to hold regional peace talks. The presentations to the different presidents were carefully planned, and women from all three countries were present at each meeting. Liberia's President Charles Taylor agreed to recall the expelled ambassadors of Sierra Leone and Guinea after meeting with the delegation. Following his encounter with the group, President Lansanah Conte of Guinea commented, "You MRU women, what you are doing is the best thing that has happened [for the region] in 10 years."

In March 2002, the three presidents met in Morocco. But MARWOPNET

---

[4] Preliminary Report, Mano River Peace Network (MARWOPNET) on participation in the 25th Summit of ECOWAS Heads of state, Dakar, Senegal, December 17-21, 2001.

representatives were not there. They learned of the meeting only two days beforehand; there were no funds for the journey, and MARWOPNET was given only observer status. As Mary Brownell commented, the greatest problem was "the male mentality that says women are not supposed to be involved in these things."[5] The Moroccan talks did not solve the continuing disagreements among the Mano Union countries.

WOMEN TAKE TO THE STREETS AGAIN

In March of 2003, as the vicious fighting between government forces and those of LURD and MODEL moved closer to the coastal settlements, Liberian women moved into action again. According to Etweda Cooper of the Liberian Women's Initiative, solidarity developed when the Muslim Women of Peace network reached out to the Christian women to "bring sense" to this whole thing. Also, a new generation of anti-war demonstrators joined the old. The Liberian Women in Peace-building Network (WIPNET), led by Leymah Gbowee, included hundreds of women from refugee camps near Monrovia.

Women in white take to the streets in Monrovia.

On Friday, April 11, about 1,000 women, dressed in white, launched a campaign against the continuing war. Many of the women from WIPNET had walked long distances to be at the meeting at City Hall. The rally was charged with emotion. While government representatives were not present to receive their petition, the women made sure it was publicized. "We are fed up," the women declared. In their statement they set forth a three-point program: an immediate ceasefire, dialogue among the opposing parties, and international monitoring of the ceasefire.

The statement was distributed widely to the government and the two rebel factions. They declared that this was only the beginning of their action and, true to their word, only a few days later they visited City Hall and occupied the parking lot so that legislators could not park their vehicles.

---

5 Quoted in Michael Fleshman, "African women struggle for a seat at the peace table," *Africa Recovery*, XVI, 4, February 2003, p. 18.

AP/Wide World Photo: Schalk van Zuydam

Calling for dialogue, WIPNET's Leymah Gbowee argued:

> It is women and children, the weaker vessels of the human race, that are most affected during and after civil conflicts. Women and children die from a combination of factors: bullets, hunger, childbirth, rape.

Displaced women told of their experiences: "Even as I speak," [said] an internally displaced person from Jahtondo town, "I can't give account of my three children. We can no longer sit and watch our children dying." Another said, "I have not seen this child's father.... I was pregnant for her when I left Tubmanburg. But I have not seen her father. I am still running," she added, and burst into tears.[6]

Starting in April, WIPNET organized women to sit in at the airfield in Sinkor, opposite the fish market, and soon others were sitting in towns around the country. At a press conference, they said:

> We feel that either we are not being listened to or we are not being taken seriously. We are *very serious* [emphasis theirs]. The Liberian women have always said that we want an immediate and unconditional ceasefire. We want all belligerent parties to disarm, and we want to see a mechanism in place that can lead to lasting and sustainable peace.

They demanded a neutral international force so that refugees could go home; they wanted "free and fair elections."[7]

In the weeks leading up to peace negotiations between the government and the two rebel groups in June 2003 women continued to press for peaceful solutions to the Liberian crisis. In a May 21st interview with the BBC, LWI Secretary General Etweda Cooper, warned of the looming humanitarian disaster that stalked the capital city and its thousands of refugees from the countryside:

> Monrovia does not have the infrastructure to accommodate the displaced that are coming. We don't have running water and electricity and basically the countryside is being captured, and therefore we will have problems with food coming into Monrovia.[8]

---

[6] "Liberian Women Call for Cessation of Hostilities and Peace Talks," Agence France Presse, April 11, 2003.

[7] "Help Restore Peace to Liberia," press release, Liberian Women Mass Action for Peace, May 31, 2003. www.peacewomen.org

[8] The NEWS/All Africa Global Media via COMTEX, May 22, 2003.

A two-day consultation of women leaders at Monrovia City Hall, organized by MARWOPNET and opened by Mary Brownell on May 27-28, focused on building consensus and a common position on how to end the political-military quagmire and reach peace. Also on May 28th, the Coalition of Women of Political Parties in Liberia – women executives of each of nine political parties – called for an immediate ceasefire and an international stabilization force that would remain in Liberia not less than three years. WIPNET and other groups continued nonviolent actions. Women in white demonstrated outside the United States Embassy seeking a U.S.-led international stabilization force.

PEACE TALKS AT LAST

Formal peace talks in Akosombo and Accra began on June 3rd, although many delegates and civil society representatives, including women, had arrived in Ghana for earlier talks. The new talks lasted for two and a half months from June 4th until August 18th, when the peace agreement was signed, and on August 21st a transitional government was approved, to be installed October 15th. Throughout this period, as delegates meeting in Ghana talked about a ceasefire and peace, conditions deteriorated in Liberia. Fighting expanded in the Liberian countryside and in the capital, Monrovia, among rebel and government forces. Death and suffering, destruction, danger and hunger grew, and women, often endangered and confronted with killers and rapists, continued their protests and their appeals for help. They were indomitable.

Women took leading roles both inside and outside the negotiation halls. The Liberia Chapter of MARWOPNET had participated in the ECOWAS peace talks at Akosombo in July and August. Led by Ruth Sando Perry, former head of state, and Theresa Leigh-Sherman, vice president of MARWOPNET, the delegation of eight was the only women's group accredited to the conference in Accra.[9]

On the day the peace talks opened under ECOWAS auspices, the Movement for Democratic Change in Liberia, headed by Nohn Rebecca Kidau, addressed an open letter to the former Nigerian Head of State, retired General Abdulsalami Abubakar, chair of the talks. The letter thanked the International Contact Group on Liberia for sponsoring the peace talks, registered concern over the manner of selection of delegates and set out recommendations about security and governance. It also expressed very deep concern over the absence of civil society from the talks:

---

[9] MARWOPNET press release, August 29, 2003

> We are incensed and further taken aback by this action, which reminds us of the arrangements preceding the 1997 elections that resulted in Liberia's woeful status today. This shameful action comes against the backdrop of a glaring reality that it is Liberian civilians who are dying, falling sick, going hungry and suffering.[10]

The women who attended the talks set forth their own declaration, "Cry Out for Peace," on June 7th. They spoke forcefully:

> The Liberian peace process faces a crisis as violence intensifies on the streets of Monrovia. The ray of hope presented by the peace talks dims with every moment. All sides in the conflict seem determined to let guns do the talking.

Calling for an immediate ceasefire, they appealed to the UN Security Council for the immediate intervention and the protection of a peacekeeping force and urged the establishment of a caretaker government, if necessary, that would disarm, demobilize, reintegrate and resettle troops, prepare the way for elections, provide humanitarian relief, work for reconciliation and restructure the army and security forces.

In a statement read on women's behalf in Akosombo in early June, Theresa Leigh-Sherman said that "the failure on the part of the United States Government and the international community to immediately intervene will leave the women with no alternative but to hold them responsible for the genocide and the humanitarian situation currently occurring in Liberia.... We, the women of Liberia, hasten to alert the world of the urgent, catastrophic situation occurring in our country."[11]

Iinternational pressure led the government of President Charles Taylor to sign a ceasefire agreement with LURD and MODEL on June 17, 2003. As it turned out, the agreement was merely the first step toward a comprehensive peace plan and a transitional government. Fighting resumed and intensified. Women persisted in their cries for peace, as *The New York Times* witnessed:

> In an empty field, in a heavy downpour in the middle of the rainy season in one of the world's wettest countries, was a small group of women, nearly all dressed in white, throwing their arms to the sky and dancing and singing drenched from head to toe, calling to God to bring an end to war. The women sang "Thank you, Jehovah, God, thank you, for you have spared my life to see this day."

---

[10] http://www.mdcl.org/abubakar.htm, June 3, 2003.

[11] Zangar, Moses M., "Liberian Women Cry Out for Peace" in *The Perspective*, Atlanta Georgia, June 11, 2003.

They are Liberia's peaceniks, a radical, some would say delusional breed, who for the last three months have been bent on praying on the side of the road, in sun and rain, every single day, to bring an end to the war. "We are tired, we are tired, we are tired of suffering," declared Louise M. Tucolon, 42. "So we come in the rain, we come in the sun to pray to our God. We know he will not come down. But he will pass through people to help us."

A woman prays for peace, crying out in front of rebel headquarters and calling on the LURD and the government to stop the fighting that is killing women and children.

Their prayers are practical. They want an international peacekeeping force to come now and stop the killings. "Tell our international brothers to come quickly," Ms. Tucolon said. "Even if right now, as I am speaking, if they could hear us and come right now, right now, we would be happy."

Last week, as government and rebel forces raged through town for two and a half days, killing, wounding and scattering tens of thousands of people, the Women in Peacebuilding Network, as they are called, were forced to hole up indoors.... The women in this field, church ladies joined by their Muslim sisters, have taken their vigils to Mr. Taylor's office and to the gates of the Guinean and American Embassies.... Leading them in song was a woman dressed in brown...they all sang "We Shall Overcome."[12]

WAR ESCALATES AND PEACE GROUPS INCREASE THEIR PRESSURE

The Mano River Union civil-society coalitions gained greater prominence as the peace talks sputtered on. In collaboration with some of their international partners and organizations in Guinea, Sierra Leone and Ghana, the Liberian Women's Initiative, represented by Etweda Cooper, submitted a memorandum on August 2, 2003, to the Chairman of ECOWAS, the heads of state of the four concerned countries, the president of the African Union and other executives of involved parties. They made general recommendations,

---

12 Sengupta, Somini, "In the Mud, Liberia's Gentlest Rebels Pray for Peace," *The New York Times,* July 1, 2003.

such as demobilization of child soldiers, and specific recommendations addressed to the articles in the draft peace agreement. Then, on August 3rd, Liberian Church and civil society leaders, women among them, held an emergency consultation in Accra.

The women's position was clarified and strengthened at the Golden Tulip Hotel in Accra at a one-day meeting on August 15th of 45 women's groups attending the peace talks. It was organized by MARWOPNET, Liberian women's organizations and UNIFEM. The result was the Golden Tulip Declaration in which the Liberian Women said they would work toward "the inclusion of women within all existing and proposed institutions including all components of the current and incoming Liberian Government...and within all structures to lead the post-conflict peace-building process."[13]

The declaration also recalled UN Security Council Resolution 1325 of October 31, 2000, the landmark United Nations "recognition of women's contributions to the maintenance and promotion of peace and security, and their specific needs and concerns in armed conflict and its aftermath, as well as the responsibilities of the international community to provide effective responses...."[14]

When ECOWAS peacekeepers arrived in Monrovia at the beginning of August the fighters in Liberia engaged in a "frenzy of rape." Rebels and government soldiers, some aged 12 or even younger, assaulted thousands of girls and women. The female population – from age 8 to age 65 – was seen as booty to be taken before the peacekeepers took over. Many of the assaults were accompanied by the murder of male relatives, victims said. "Wild-eyed men" went from door to door, killing and raping. In one incident, gunmen burst into a home and raped a 10-year-old child on her birthday "leaving her lying in a pool of blood and vomit – dead." Her mother, Rebecca, was smashed on the head with a hammer and had her clothes torn off. About her daughter, Rebecca said, the man "raped her to death.'" A 14-year old friend was raped in the same house.[15]

At last, a peace agreement was signed in Accra on August 18th by the Government of Liberia, LURD, MODEL and 18 political parties. Because of the critical mediation role MARWOPNET played among the various factions involved in the peace talks, the network was one of the signatories witnessing the agreement. During the two months of their stay in Ghana the delegation lobbied to put forward their peace agenda as included in the Abuja Plan

---

[13] http://www.peacewomen.org/news/1325News/issue30.html#Statement.

[14] "Report of the Secretary-General on women, peace and security," S/2002/1154, para 3, United Nations, October 16, 2002.

[15] Zavis, Alexandra, The Associated Press, August 10, 2003.

of Action adopted in May 2000 by the women of the Mano River countries.[16]

This and other actions toward regional peace and security led the president of the United Nations General Assembly to select MARWOPNET in 2003 as one of six recipients of the prestigious United Nations Prize in the Field of Human Rights. The president stated:

> The network has brought an effective multi-dimensional, coordinated and regional approach to the struggle for human rights through initiatives to restore peace and to ensure that women's voices are included at all levels of the decision-making process. It has been active at both the grass-roots level and the highest levels of government, successfully bringing the heads of state of their three countries back to the negotiating table in 2001, and as a delegate, mediator and signatory to the Liberian peace talks in August 2003.[17]

Sarah Daraba Kaba of the Mano River Women Peace Network receives the 2003 UN Human Rights Prize from Julian Robert Hunte of Saint Lucia, President of the 58th session of the General Assembly.

AUGUST 21, 2003: ANOTHER STEP TOWARD A NEW LIBERIA

Charles Taylor had been pressured into exile in Nigeria on August 11th, handing over the presidency to his deputy, Moses Blah. The peace talks, which had begun June 4th, culminated on August 21st with the selection of an inter-

---

[16] MARWOPNET press release, August 29, 2003.
[17] Announcement of the awardees of the 2003 UN Prize in the Field of Human Rights, United Nations, NY, December 2, 2003.

im chairman for the transitional government to remain until 2006, when elections were to be held. Gyude Bryant was chosen from among three candidates by an "electoral college" – the three warring parties, i.e., the Taylor government, LURD and MODEL. Three candidates had been selected by political parties and civil society groups from among 11 seeking the position. Actually, Ellen Johnson-Sirleaf was the favorite among the trio, having received 33 votes from the political parties and NGOs. Second was Rudolph Sherman, with 18 votes, and Bryant broke a tie for third. Sirleaf, expressing pride about the "overwhelming support" she received from the parties and NGOs, told journalists that she intends to work inside Liberia, not as a government official but in areas of her expertise.[18] Following the election, Bryant asked Sirleaf to chair a commission on good governance.

Near the end of August, women still felt compelled to protest:

> Women dressed in white t-shirts to symbolize peace marched on West African peace forces' headquarters in driving rain...pleading for faster deployment into Liberia's still-unsettled and starving interior. The roughly 100 women...waved rain-wilted signs with slogans urging *Total peace, not half peace*, *War everyday* and *Our sisters in Liberia are dying....* "We want peace, no more war," the women chanted.... "We're asking them to speedily deploy to the countryside to stop the killing of our people," said Leymah Gbowee, 31, a march organizer [and head of WIPNET].[19]

The United Nations Security Council approved 15,000 peacekeepers on September 9th – the second largest UN peacekeeping mission in the world, after Sierra Leone. They were to replace the ECOWAS contingent that was the first to arrive after the peace accords. The UN Mission in Liberia (UNMIL) came into being on October 1, 2003, two weeks before the transitional government of Gyude Bryant took power on October 15th. UNMIL is charged with enforcing the August 18th peace agreement and helping the new transitional government assert its authority in the country.

As we write the final words of this book, in December 2003, the situation in Liberia is hopeful but remains unstable. Cholera has broken out in major cities, and fighting continues in the countryside. The United Nations warns that as many as 15,000 child soldiers conscripted to fight for government and rebel movements must be reintegrated in civil society; 70 percent of the warring factions are under age 18. The more than 200,000 people who fled to Monrovia in June and July did not escape the violence. According to a United Nations report, about 250,000 persons are believed to have died in war-relat-

---

[18] Dukulé, Abdoulaye W., "Liberia Negotiations End, Armed Factions Tap Transition Leader," All Africa.com, August 21, 2003, http://allafrica.com/stories/200308210225.html.
[19] The Associated Press, August 28, 2003.

ed situations between 1989 and 2003.[20] Eighty percent of Liberians now live in abject poverty.

The road to genuine peace is bound to be rocky, but it is certain that women will be vigilant monitors and, hopefully, leaders of the process.

DEFINING A NATIONAL AGENDA FOR WOMEN

In their study, *Women, War, Peace,*[21] Elisabeth Rehn and Ellen Johnson-Sirleaf conclude that the only way African women can become equal partners in peace is to support their struggles for full participation in national political, economic and social life. This is a worldwide issue. Official statements at the Fourth World Conference on Women at Beijing, China, in 1995[22] and the 1999 assessment of progress made in Liberia in implementing the Beijing Platform for Action[23] document the under-representation of women in decision-making roles, not only in civil society organizations but also in government and other authority structures.

As Amos Sawyer, chair of the Center of Democratic Empowerment, emphasized in 1998:

> It is in the interest of all of us, man and woman alike, to look at our development and determine that women's participation, women's empowerment, is a critical element in moving the society forward. Empowerment of women is part of the process of building peace. We must not see peace as one set of activities and empowerment as another...empowerment is nothing more than broadening the base of participation...promoting democracy, promoting economic advancement, promoting social justice...through economic advancement of women, through political involvement of women. It is all of these that will give us the ultimate peace that we are talking about.

Women gained space and recognition for their activities between 1990 and 1997, and they continue to employ the highly successful advocacy and lobbying strategies that they developed. The appointment of a female head of

---

[20] UN Office for the Coordination of Humanitarian Affairs, IRINNews.org, "Liberia: Security Council approves 15,000 peacekeepers," September 19, 2003: http://www.irinnews.org/report.asp?ReportID=36719&SelectRegion=West_Africa&SelectCountry=LIBERIA.

[21] *Women, War, Peace: The Independent Experts' Assessment on the Impact of Armed Conflict on Women and Women's Role in Peace-building,* Volume 1 in *Progress of the World's Women 2002,* UNIFEM, New York, January 2003.

[22] Vera R. Gibson, *Liberia: A Country Report on the Status of Women,* May 5, 1994.

[23] *The Beijing+5 Liberia Country Report on Gender Equality and Women's Empowerment,* Monrovia, Republic of Liberia, September 24, 1999.

state in 1996 encouraged them to envision active participation in reconstruction. However, it became clear that one woman in a position of power could not provide the equal mainstreaming of women and gender issues that women in Liberia seek. Now they desire deeper involvement in their country's economic, social and political life.

Weade Kobbah Wureh, former vice chairperson of the Council of State of the Liberian Transitional Government, reflects their determination, asserting:

> I don't think peace achieved through the blood, sweat and tears, humiliation and destruction of lives and property should be just thrown to others to carry it any way they see fit. Inasmuch as [we] participated and…sacrificed for peace, it's incumbent on all of us to work towards managing that peace.

Liberian women have had the right to vote since 1944. Yet they have a low participation rate in government positions at all levels. In the Beijing+5 report of 1999, Liberia reported that women held only 2 percent of ministerial positions; 5 percent of legislative seats and 1 percent of other executive positions. Lower levels of literacy (22 percent female vs. 54 percent male) and attendance at primary and secondary schools (40 percent & 32 percent girls vs. 60 percent & 68 percent boys) are a major barrier to girls' and women's decision-making access.[24]

Women waiting for Gyude Bryant's plane and the start of his transitional government told the photographer it is better to say something and risk being persecuted or killed than to sit around waiting to be killed without speaking up.

The Beijing Platform for Action and the UN Convention on the Elimination of All Forms of Discrimination Against Women (CEDAW), ratified by Liberia in 1998, and UN Security Council Resolution 1325 of 2000 provide important policy frameworks for women's ongoing peace-building and social reconstruction initiatives. While the government's declining revenue base has limited progress on addressing the institutional mechanisms and other priorities of the Beijing Platform for Action, UNIFEM,

---

[24] *Ibid.*

UNDP, other UN and international partners have provided funding for projects to integrate critical gender concerns into national reconstruction programming by the government or NGOs. A positive step was taken in 2001 when the Ministry of Gender and Development was established by law, and Dorothy Musuleng Cooper was nominated and chosen for the post of Minister of Gender and Development.

As Etweda Cooper says:

> Liberian women have proven themselves to be skilled and astute managers of the local economy; they have shown that they are capable to playing important roles in war and peace and are skilled in diplomacy when needed.... Our challenges are now to ensure that real empowerment of women is on the national agenda.... We shall have to exert ourselves in ensuring that transformation. For it is much easier to speak of transformation than to achieve it – and the costs [are] high.

At the same time untold numbers of Liberian women are trying to make peace with the horrors they lived through, as *The New York Times* reports:[25]

Kula, a 47-year-old rape victim, at a center for women traumatized by war. Photographed in shadow for fear of reprisals, Kula was repeatedly gang-raped by rebels, including one she guesses was no older than ten.

War made women the spoils of conquest, not unlike sacks of rice and four-wheel-drive vehicles. But what stands out is that in the succession of conflicts in Liberia since 1989, many women, and sometimes the same women, were raped by fighters from all sides.

They were raped when Mr. Taylor was a rebel leader fighting his way to the presidency. They were raped when the next band of rebels fought to oust him. They have been raped since Mr. Taylor's departure on August 11th, as his loyalists and enemies continue to fight in remote jungle outposts far from areas patrolled by 4,000 United Nations peacekeepers.

The scale of the problem is impossible to ascertain precisely in a country where everything has been destroyed. But anecdotal evidence suggests that 14 years of intermittent warfare crushed many traditional sanctions, unleashing conduct unthinkable in normal times. Mothers and daughters were raped by the same men. Boys assaulted women old enough to be their mothers.

---

[25] Somini Sengupta, "All Sides in Liberian Conflict Make Women Spoils of War," *The New York Times*, November 20, 2003.

Rebuilding the social fabric is among the toughest challenges facing Liberia's transitional government. That government is made up of the very warring factions that are accused of atrocities, and it remains to be seen how it will respond to the competing demands of reconciliation and redress.

The chairman of the unity government, C. Gyude Bryant, has said nothing publicly about how war crimes will be punished, but some human rights advocates are calling on the United Nations mission here to support a commission of inquiry....

So far, the courts in this country have hardly provided recourse. The stigma of rape still makes it s a crime that most women here find too difficult to speak of.

POSTSCRIPT: LEARNING FROM LIBERIAN WOMEN

This book has captured only a fraction of Liberian women's pioneering, often courageous and always sustained work for the alleviation of the suffering of their people through humanitarian aid, peace education and mediation among warring factions to end the conflict. During the interim peace of the later 1990s, before the relapse into conflict, they helped to reintegrate young soldiers into society, care for orphans and widows, counsel rape victims and resettle war-affected populations.

Early in the fighting the women's immediate reaction was to feed, comfort, heal and harbor refugees, especially children. Individually they bravely faced armed and trigger-happy soldiers, some only children, and used their persuasive powers and status as mothers, wives, sisters and grandmothers. That tactic was successful surprisingly often during the protracted conflict.

Empowered by individual success and increasingly impatient with what was essentially a man's war (even though some women joined), women soon focused on the political aspects of peace and decided that organization is key to political action. The women's organizations joined forces – rural with urban, Christian with Muslim – and created an umbrella group, the Liberian Women's Initiative (LWI), whose overwhelming concern was peace. They took to the streets, sent faxes, negotiated with soldiers – again and again. Later they translated their unity into a subregional network of women peace activists in the Mano River Union countries of Liberia, Sierra Leone and Guinea, calling it MARWOPNET – the Mano River Women's Peace Network.

Emboldened by mutual support, the women courageously worked to take part in the ECOWAS-sponsored peace talks in West Africa, lobbying and mediating with the warring factions and other delegates to advocate peace and press for its urgency until they were finally recognized and welcomed. They successfully conducted mediation seminars that brought the major warring groups together. They never ceased demonstrating in public places, in drizzling rain and burning sun, calling for "war no more."

Their success in putting the horrors and destruction of the many-sided civil war in the faces of the fighters and attracting the international press to their country's plight was outstanding. Historians should give them credit together with the religious leaders and groups, of which women were also a part.

Yet the women were unable to penetrate the final peace talks, other than as official observers, and then only a handful of women, from MARWOPNET, were allowed in.[26] And while the peace talks painfully progressed, the warring parties engaged in a "frenzy of rape" in Monrovia and elsewhere, taking their last revenge before the ECOWAS peacekeepers arrived.

As they spoke of their peacemaking activities, the women of Liberia offered these lessons from their experiences:
   ✓ Above all, listen.
   ✓ Be neutral.
   ✓ Be honest so that you will be trusted.
   ✓ Be patient.
   ✓ Know yourself.
   ✓ Be committed to peace; carry peace with you.
   ✓ Set aside jealousies.
   ✓ Be strong and courageous in your convictions and actions.
   ✓ Practice negotiating skills.
   ✓ Approach all parties with courtesy and ethics.
   ✓ Work to build consensus among yourselves, the peacemakers.
   ✓ Be prepared to dialogue and not fight with opposing parties.
   ✓ Draw on your knowledge of traditions and include among the peace-makers those who understand the cultures of those you are meeting.
   ✓ Look for common ground among those in conflict.
   ✓ Bring humanitarian relief when you come to talk peace.
   ✓ Open doors for self-help and economic recovery.

WHAT IF...

We need to ask "what if" about women's potentially far greater involvement and influence in peacemaking:

---

[26] MARWOPNET press release, August 29, 2003.

For Liberians:

What if women's insistence, and that of other civil society groups, that disarmament precede elections in 1996, had been honored?

What if women, with their stories of violence and destruction and death and their knowledge and use of conciliation techniques, had been present in significant numbers as delegates at the early peace talks to counter the power struggles that typify the trade-off approach of warring parties?

What if the income from Liberia's natural riches – gold, diamonds, rubber, timber – were spent on education and training, health services, access roads and expanded markets for all Liberians?

For everyone:

What if it was widely known and accepted that international law now stipulates that rape is a crime of genocide and those guilty would be prosecuted?

What if the international community honored the provisions of Security Council Resolution 1325, to recognize "women's contributions to the maintenance and promotion of peace and security, and their specific needs and concerns in armed conflict and its aftermath, as well as the responsibilities of the international community to provide effective responses"?

What if every boy and girl had an alternative to "playing war": access to education through secondary school and opportunities for wage- or self-employment?

Liberian children hold placards at the October 2003 launch of Working With Our Children, an organization formed by women to promote, advocate and protect children's rights.

What if the world's women joined hands to campaign for peace – for days, months and years without killing?

We cannot know for sure *what if*, but we, and people everywhere, have much to learn from the heroic quest of Liberian women for peace – peace now and peace forever more.

AP/WWP/EPA Photo: Ahmed Allanzo

The UN estimates as many as 15,000 child soldiers will have to be reintegrated into Liberian society.

In December 2003, former fighters begin turning in their weapons to UN peacekeepers.

Top three photos: Pewee Flomoku courtesy of Andrew Carlson. Bottom: The UN Office for the Coordination of Humanitarian Affairs at www.irinnews.org

Part III:
INSIGHTS FROM EXPERIENCE:
SIXTEEN PEACE PEOPLE SPEAK[1]

Mary N. Brownell, President, Liberian Women's Initiative

We the women were actually the victims of this civil crisis in Liberia. Women were engaged in the relief effort and started the organization Women in Action. But I said that we the women should do a little more than that because there were still atrocities all around. We wanted the war to stop. And so this wild thought came to me that instead of sitting down and saying the men should play the major role because they were the ones who brought about this war, if our voices joined together as one we could make an impact on the Liberian society and the international community.

With this purpose in mind, I talked with Dr. Evelyn Kandakai, who is now the Minister of Education, about us getting together and forming a pressure group and a movement. She thought that was a very good idea. So I invited a few women to meet here at my hall, and after a lot of brainstorming they got the vision. We did not want to limit it to just the few of us who were at this meeting, so we called a mass meeting in February 1994 for women from all walks of life. We decided to present our first position statement to the government and to send it to the international community, United Nations, OAU, ECOWAS. We wanted to tell them how the women felt, that we were being victimized, and we wanted redress, and the only way was for them to talk to our warlords at that time, to stop the fighting in Liberia.

And so we continued from there, using all the strategies we could think about to make our voices heard. We demonstrated on the streets of Monrovia. We visited almost all the African countries wherever there was a peace conference going on. We carried letters and hand delivered them to the different warlords, appealing to them as their mothers and sisters to stop this fighting because it was Liberians killing Liberians. There was a time when we decided to go to Bomi Hills. OK, we planned, chartered buses, and went.

We met the fighters on Po River Bridge. We got down from the bus trying to reach to them, the fellow looked up and down at me and said, "Look, if you know what I know, you better get in your bus and get back to Monrovia. Otherwise I will spray you and your women." You know we were just like

---

[1] All interviews were conducted in Liberia between 1998 and 1999.

those country dogs; we got back in our buses and came back to Monrovia. How did those boys know we were coming, to have been on the bridge to stop us? Someone gave them that information that I was bringing those women up there.

The goals of the Liberian Women's Initiative were first, disarmament. We also felt that nobody should become president of Liberia through the barrel of the gun: the person should go to the polls. If the Liberian people had the confidence to elect that person as president, fine, we will cooperate with the person. We talked about education and the reunification of the country.... We stressed free and fair elections. These were the four things we set out to do, and by the grace of God we were able to accomplish them to a great, great extent.

Mary Brownell

We connected ourselves with other groups advocating the same thing, like the Inter-Faith Mediation Council, the Justice and Peace Commission of the Catholic Secretariat and the council of chiefs, and we met regularly at the Catholic secretariat at least once a week to plan our strategies. We worked with interest groups, [such as] Dr. Tipoteh and his people. We met regularly and discussed issues. Members of political parties came into our meetings also. So we worked together as a team and whenever there was a position statement I always read it on behalf of the women.

We were involved with other African women. For instance, I was fortunate to attend peace conferences in Dakar, in Beijing, in Rwanda, in South Africa. When we met at these conferences and began to share experiences, what the women had to go through with their sons and daughters, you know, and believe me when I heard those stories, it's just like a replaying of what took place in my country. There was a time in South Africa when I became very emotional. I told them, "We didn't expect you to take guns and come and fight our battle, but at least to hear on the BBC or to get some letter of encouragement to say we, the African women, we are with you, we identify with you." I said, "This would mean more to us than for us as African women to just travel around, discussing peace and discussing peace and discussing peace." And I think they bought that message because it took no time after that before we had a team composed of African women going around to different African countries, especially when there was conflict, trying to give their support to the women.

It is so easy to destroy and very, very hard to build up. We still have a long way to go. That is why the Liberian Women's Initiative has undertaken this

Photo courtesy of Musue Haddad

peace seminar, Bridges of Peace, going to different villages and talking to our people there about how we can reconcile with one another even though it's hard…. The only thing was that the women had hoped that LWI would be in the position to give them some seed money to do business themselves. It is a very good idea. If I can get the funding, I would like to go back to those neighborhoods or communities. We will pursue this.

Peace can actually be built. First, we have to establish confidence in ourselves. We have to establish confidence in our leaders, who must play a major role. We don't want them to just talk peace, we want them to practice peace. Nobody can say you have peace, peace of mind, if you are hungry, if you don't have food to eat, you do not know where the next meal is coming from, or how your children will go to school…. These are problems that we have to tackle.

Peacemaking is the responsibility of every citizen. We can't leave it to one or two persons. That's what brought about this war…. Every Liberian was a victim of what happened. So everybody, all Liberians have to play a role if we really want to have peace.

Ruth Caesar, Ministry of Planning and Economic Affairs

So far as I'm concerned, all my activity since 1990 has been peace. Even giving someone a cup of water is peace. If you sit down with a group of women to discuss their problems, that is peace. If you share your meal with another family who come into the displaced camp you are in, that's peace. If you talk to a young girl who was raped, that's peace. That's my way of life. Women cannot develop outside of peace.

My own area of involvement was at the level of my job, where I had to mobilize women and chair meetings that established the groups that went to conferences. They were not placed on government delegations, so we worked out strategies to mobilize funds. I personally never had the opportunity to go to any conferences but was involved in formulating the resolutions and the statements that were presented to ECOWAS leaders.

I looked at myself as a trailblazer, and I looked at my work as a God-given responsibility. I remember when we formed the committee for the women to visit the faction leaders. I would go find people's homes, especially those of the rural women that were on this committee, tell them when the meeting was to be held. But I don't want to take the credit here because it is the women, collectively, who have the credit. We all did according to our own capabilities.

We had a lot of support. The minister, Mrs. Amelia Ward, gave a lot of support. The women leaders helped to facilitate. You had the block from the Women's Initiative – they were resourceful. Even Madam Ruth Perry would come to the Planning Ministry if she missed a meeting and say, "Keep up the good work – I'm behind you." You had Madam Annie Saydee who was the Sapo [people's] governor. We all put our hands together.

We encouraged women to go an extra mile, getting everybody involved as much as possible. Everybody that came – market women, rural women who couldn't speak English – was welcomed. We put our arms around them. I would go to communities, sit down with the women in their houses and find out their problems. The strategy was showing care for people, telling them they too are part of the peace process. And so in our meetings you saw rural women…. We made them feel relaxed and comfortable so much that they

Ruth Caesar

were able to articulate what they wanted. During the time of elections, the same women went to their counties to sensitize women to vote.

I am very proud of the Liberian women, especially the indigenous women. The average rural woman now knows about peace. She's empowered. What surprised me was the establishment of the Liberia Rural Women's Association. Those women had their elections according to the Robert's Rules of Order, and even yesterday they invited me to their meeting and conducted it in very simple English. They had a motion; it was not in flowery or sophisticated words. They are working now toward establishing a banking system for rural women.

The strategies that we decided upon, like forming groups to go from village to village, were formulated in consensus with women leaders and discussed at workshops. For different things you need different strategies. For example, when things were tough and we wanted disarmament before elections, we marched. We mobilized those who felt comfortable; we didn't force anybody. Those who went to Abuja lobbied the heads of state. In fact, we started to lobby from here by telephone to their embassies and their state capitals. Old lady Mary Brownell was very instrumental in that.

We formed a delegation consisting of all elements of women: rural women, rural women leadership, urban women, urban women leadership, lawyers, a motherly figure; they visited each faction leader so they [the faction leaders] said, "Well, if we are going to meet together, we will meet under the leadership of the women." Women met [the faction leaders] in their homes. From what I understand, Theresa Leigh-Sherman would have her bag packed, and when her phone rang and they said, "Come, Mr. Warring Faction A can see you immediately," she picked up her bag. She was ever ready.

We have learned that peace is very expensive – expensive in that you have to give a lot to get peace and you have to learn to respect people and value human life. You have to develop a habit of accepting that in a negotiation you can get not everything you want but what you need in order to acquire peace. In other words, we have learned that to negotiate for peace is a give and take.

There were limitations. We had this great divide between greater Liberia and lesser Liberia. As much as our hearts yearned to reach out to the women in the other counties, we were afraid of each other. Everybody had their own loyalties, and this limited us because the women united would have had a greater force. But when we looked at the time constraint and the danger, the loss of lives and property and continuous warfare, we went ahead and utilized what we had.

We still need to work on our attitudes. We still need to be realistic. Some people still think that there are losers and there are winners. And the winners are still behaving like winners after a marathon: they want to take all the glory. We have come to see that this was not a winner and a loser thing. This was a situation where we all lost.

Dorothy Musuleng Cooper, educator, former Foreign Minister

As I reflect on my life as an individual and then on my work with the Peace Corps and with teacher training, I think I've always been involved in peace building and conflict resolution. I've done that as an educational administrator working with the people in the community and schools, teachers. I've also done that in the community where we've lived, between families, among children. During the war I've had to be a go-between between combatants and citizens.

On and off we were involved in peace talks. But the major one was in Geneva in 1993 where the document was developed that was taken to Cotonou and became the Cotonou Accords. I had the opportunity to be on the team with others from other factions, and sometimes when the relationships broke down, we served as intermediaries to reestablish channels. The first Council of State evolved out of that.

In 1994 I was selected to go to the Akosombo workshop, a training for agents of peace and reconciliation. The group included a broad-based selection of

Liberians from military factions, from the judiciary, from the private and public sectors. Some of the strategies that we used are really essential to peace building. For instance, when we spoke openly at first about our own perceptions of why we had the problem, there were all kinds of accusations, finger-pointing and aggressive statements. We had to become sensitive to the fact that for the individual the statements were true and real, they were a perception, a conditioning. Then each group, each individual had to divulge their own perceptions about the issues, and we categorized those issues and began to deal with them as a group instead of as individuals. That was a lot of work. Then we had to talk about each other, how we interacted and how those immediate impressions could or could not affect peace and the establishment of confidence and communication channels. So it was a long week, very intensive.

The organization we formed there was called (although we're a little bit dormant now), LIPCORE, the Liberian Initiative for Peace and Conflict Resolution. Did we accomplish any of our objectives? Yes we did. We returned home, organized ourselves and made a list of people as well as groups and institutions that we wanted to make contact with. Then we used the approach of an intermediary, a mediator, and we would go in and say to somebody who hadn't participated in this group's development: "We would like to come and see you and members of your group, and I would like to be the one to bring my teammates because you know and have confidence in me, and I know them." We had a lot of success, then gradually there was a break in the process. When you come out into the greater community, if the group does not remain together, the semblance of security, confidence, camaraderie begins to disintegrate. Our successes were that we were able to break the barriers of communication and interaction among the various groups – the warring factions – and establish a new approach.

Work with LIPCORE was a group approach, but we still had to work as individuals. I had a pickup and we went around collecting people, being there as a buffer between them and the fighters, serving as a confidence center and helping them to reestablish their lives in other parts of the country. At Cuttington College, we had to evacuate the campus when the fighting was getting closer to us.

I had a harrowing experience where I had to go in and directly intervene. Mrs. Mason, the wife of the president of Cuttington, was threatened by one of Prince Johnson's fighters and all of the people in her house were held at gunpoint for some time. I went into that situation to confront the fighter, sit between him and Mrs. Mason and over a three-hour period talk him out of harming her or destroying their home. "You have no mother, this woman is older than you are, she hasn't really done anything to you, why do you want to kill her?" Because we stayed and were constant, we didn't threaten him and eventually we talked him out of his purpose and he got into a vehicle, and he left.

Clara d'Almeida, entrepreneur

My first experience [with peace building] was in 1992. At that time people were trying to organize different political parties. I understood that a former classmate was part of LPC [Liberia Peace Council], so I got in touch with her and started talking to her about the evil happening to people. It didn't make sense to start something else when we were trying to unite people. That's when I really got into peace activities. At that time the women's group had not formed, but we went from one faction leader to another. Then we tried to bring them together to discuss where next to go. It was me, Theresa Sherman and Evelyn Townsend around 1994.

With the faction ULIMO-J's split, the first thing we did was to build confidence from both sides. It took months to gain the confidence of the two groups, but they trusted us because they saw that we were not taking sides. We were not members of any organization except the women's group. We were not telling John Brown what Peter Paul said. No, that was not our business. Our business was to try to get all of them together.... From there we could start working on how to get them to town. That was the main objective – bringing them to town, for once we got them to town they wouldn't fight Monrovia. When you are in a glass house you don't throw stones. That's how we went about it for all the other groups too. Then we tried to get all the warlords, factions together at a conference at the National Bank. It took months, six months to a year to get to that point.

At the end of the [bank meeting], the faction leaders softened their positions. To me that was the breaking point because that was the first time that they all met in one place and were able to take a decision. One thing we told them when getting them together was that there would be no publicity, and everybody had to practically take an oath that whatever happened in that room stayed in that room. So there was secrecy. We didn't want the newspapers getting in the way, trying to make anybody look like a hero. Nobody was going to hear what you had to say, so you might as well just sit and tell the truth, sit and say exactly what you wanted to say.

Sani Abacha hosted the May 1995 ECOWAS Mediation Committee Conference [at Abuja]. The Council of State wanted delegates from the women with them as representatives from the Liberia Government, but most women said no. They had always been this neutral body, and it was this neutrality that caused the faction heads to trust them. So we decided to go on our own instead. The Council of State refused to give us any money so we begged for tickets. The women had asked Mrs. Brownell, Theresa Leigh-Sherman and Evelyn Townsend to go. But Mrs. Brownell decided that she was going to go with the Council of State, as a government delegate, so I was asked to go. The three of us went.

Now the beautiful part about it. We carried a presentation – a picture of what was happening in Liberia – because the conferences were only listening to what the warlords had to say, but the women and children are the most vulnerable in war. When we got there we went to the ECOWAS building and asked how we could put our names on the program to speak. The secretary told us that we could not because it was never done. They had already finished making their program, and besides individuals could not come in. I saw Dr. Banana and he said, "Oh, it's never been done before. You Liberian women, what do you want this for?"

> Ask anybody who was in Nigeria: They will tell you Nigeria stood still for an hour because every station focused on Liberian women presenting their hearts.

Then a friend of mine said, "Try and talk to the ECOWAS secretary, Eduardo Benjamin." I called him in his hotel room. So at two o'clock we went upstairs. We sat and explained some of the atrocities that the people – we the women and the children – were going through. Benjamin sat there and cried. He said, "Well I cannot promise you people...but...President Rawlings is coming in and it's his conference. I will talk to him and hear what he will say. If he agrees, I will call you." But the hotel we were in had no telephone, it was just one of these fleabags. Three women slept in just one big bed; that's all we could afford, and we hadn't had any food to eat so what can I tell him? We showed him where the hotel was so he said, "Okay, I will send somebody to you." The night passed and we didn't hear anything.

In the morning we went to the opening of the conference where everybody made their big speech and everything was supposed to happen. Then President Rawlings said, "I beg your indulgence for me to do something very unorthodox. There's a group of people we have never heard from. And these are most vulnerable in this whole thing, the women and the children of Liberia." Ask anybody who was in Nigeria: They will tell you Nigeria stood still for an hour because every station focused on Liberian women presenting their hearts.

Every time I talk about it tears come to my eyes. The men and women in that hall cried because they had never heard that story told. The only thing they were hearing about is who wants to rule, who wants to do this, but what they were doing, the atrocities going on, they never heard about them.... And that's when the whole conference made a turn, and it became a different conference. It focused now on the atrocities that were happening. The next [peace] meeting that was held, we were invited. We were now recognized as people who had something important to say – more than washing dishes and taking care of children.

When you deal in such matters you should be honest. Be honest with yourself and be honest with the people who you are coming to – let the honesty begin with you. You have to be neutral. If you find out that you cannot be neutral, then stay out of it and let somebody else take it over. The most important step to lasting peace is to try to satisfy the people. Let them be able to get their kids to where they want to be – in school. Let them be able to get up in the morning, find something to feed their children, let that man regain his manhood and be respected as a man. We have to go back to the soil.

Tiawan Gongloe, legal counselor

I worked intensely with the peace process from 1990 to 1994 when the interim government stepped down in March. As a man, I was impressed with the women who played key roles, for example Ellen Johnson-Sirleaf signed a letter to the United Nations Secretary-General with a lot of men, calling for the intervention of the United Nations in the hostilities. That was in 1990, before the Banjul [Gambia] summit of heads of state on August 6th and 7th that caused the formation of the interim government and the establishment of ECOMOG [the Economic Community of West African States' Ceasefire Monitoring Group]. Sirleaf also participated in the Banjul meeting. Miatta Fahnbulleh participated. On the other side women with NPFL [National Patriotic Front of Liberia]: Grace Minor was always in the meetings, as was Victoria Reffell.

I remember that in early September [1990] when I arrived in Liberia as a member of the advance team of the interim government, I saw Weade Kobbah-Wreh at the ECOMOG base trying to restore the newspapers and the radio stations for communication to the public. Later on Miatta Fahnbulleh produced a record calling for peace and lauding the role of ECOMOG in peacemaking. Amelia Ward, who was the first female minister with the interim government, played a very important role in harnessing international NGOs to come and provide relief.

I also remember the Lomé [Togo] meeting in February 1991. Mother Gibson and Munah Redd went there as Liberian women [not representing a women's group] to speak on behalf of women from Monrovia. They presented a paper and circulated it among the heads of state, about how Liberian women and children were suffering. They were mothers whose children were fighting; they were gathering food for their men who were hiding under the beds. They presented a very passionate story. Women were pillars of the family yet they were feeling the brunt of the war. It was a bold step because that was a period when people were afraid to speak out on issues and feared the very high cost of making statements.

During the Lomé meeting and the Yamoussoukro [Côte d'Ivoire] meeting, which followed in 1991, women's groups did not go, but women went as part of the interim government delegation or part of the NPFL delegation. They were in the shadow of men at that time so didn't feature prominently.

Later on [in 1994] Mary Brownell, Ma Mary Brownell, and some women established the Women's Initiative as a spontaneous response to the stalemate in the peace process. They held demonstrations in Monrovia, calling for the warring factions to end the war and calling for more seriousness on the part of the international community to make a genuine effort to end the war. The Women's Initiative started as a pressure group; now it is a full-fledged NGO. Mary Brownell, Comfort Sawyer, Ophelia Tate, Mother Gibson and a good number of Liberian women marched and called on the men of Liberia to be serious about peace. Their statement said war was being fought by men, but women felt the brunt.

The women's groups became much more active [in peace conferences] after 1994. One of the things about those conferences is that, unlike men, women were always out there lingering with all sides and engaging the men on all sides to soften their hearts to bring peace. They were very effective because they were not involved in high rhetoric of war in the conference hall. Many men were relaxed, talking freely with these women while they were talking diplomatically, or deceptively, with men at the conference table or even outside. They were prepared to say what was really at stake to the women, who then shared it with key negotiators in the peace process.

Speaking of the [1995] Abuja meeting where Theresa Leigh-Sherman presented the paper of the Liberian women's groups, I understand that paper went far in galvanizing the peace process because the politicians, the heads of states listened more to what the women had to say than what the conflicting parties had to say. That was a very meaningful contribution women made to the peace process.

No one will doubt Mary Brownell and Ruth Sando Perry played outstanding roles in the peace process. Mary Brownell was the lead woman who was galvanizing all the women to stand up to atrocities and the intransigence of men – speaking on national issues without fear. Ruth Sando Perry showed the trick to actually cause disarmament. It was only under her leadership [that disarmament was successful]. She played a very, very meaningful role in that respect because that was what the larger population was stressing. She kept saying there will be no election without disarmament, she galvanized public support, she held meetings at the Antoinette Tubman Stadium, and even when there was talk about safe haven elections, she opposed it: "There will be elections all over Liberia when there is disarmament."

During the two Councils of State before Perry, there was a lot of wrangling, but when she took over she was able to keep the council going, even though she disagreed with many members. The population of Liberia never lost confidence in the council headed by Perry; it lasted less than a year and achieved its purpose.

Very often [in peace negotiations] attention is focused on the warring parties and their leaders. But they must not alone be allowed to choose who should attend conferences. The facilitators must look into the country and select women to be part of the process. I think if the participation of women is made a pre-condition, ...the sooner you get them involved in the peace process, the faster you will have peace. Women speak their minds, and because they speak their minds it is easy for the negotiators to know what is at stake.... The facilitators told us that in some countries when opposing parties shake hands, then peace is nearer, but Liberians were shaking hands and drinking together and eating together and at the same time fighting war.

> I think if the participation of women is made a pre-condition, ...the sooner you get them involved in the peace process, the faster you will have peace.

As you know, during the entire war women were the only ones who were capable of moving throughout the country, and for that reason some women, I'm able to say, are braver than Liberian men. Our women were the only ones who were brave enough to come from what we call "Greater Liberia" [NPFL territories] to Monrovia, and women in Monrovia were also taking commodities that were not in "Greater Liberia," like kerosene, gasoline and imported commodities. Who were the ones that were moving produce across this country? Women! And those activities sustained them. You see a lot of men, educated or illiterate, looking for jobs. Women don't look for jobs. Most women sustain themselves outside government and company jobs, so they have built up that capacity to be independent.

Evelyn Kandakai, Minister of Education

My first experience [of peacemaking] stemmed from pre-war work with the National Adult Education Association of Liberia. After 1990, we came together and started brainstorming as to how to put NAEAL together again. We had a consultation with different NGO people and decided on a peace education program. We inaugurated the program with speakers from different backgrounds – a student and several religious leaders – talking about peace, to get into the need for peace. We worked in consultation with the African Association of Literacy and Adult Education. We had what we called a peace education extravaganza and a very successful children's peace festival, then moved with YMCA partners to displaced persons' camps around Monrovia. We took a peace theatre from the Kendeja Cultural Center. We mixed peace messages, entertainment and sports. With the assistance of UNICEF, we were also able to organize a peace education and resource center....

We had high school students' debates about the role of ECOMOG in Liberia and other questions about peace. One of the key effects was awareness-building...so we were one of the groups that brought about the environment for people to sing about peace, to talk about peace, to get involved in peace education and peacemaking.

The NAEAL sensitized me to get involved in other groups. I was sent to a meeting in Zimbabwe by the African Association and NAEAL where they talked about the pivotal role of women in peacemaking. This is where the groundwork for something like the Women's Initiative may have been planted in my psyche.

We used a lot of strategies at the Women's Initiative. One of the first is to involve not only women but a lot of women [emphasizing] that peace is everybody's business, it concerns everybody. There were some parties that were not so keen on talking, so you would go and talk to them by themselves or send delegations to talk to them. We made a lot of position statements that were very strong and caused the initiative to gain credibility too. Another development was the LDF – Liberia Disarmament Fund. I was representing the Women's Initiative. We were trying to get money together to see whether we could buy the arms from the fighters. In that particular group I worked with men. One of the lessons I learned – it was very disappointing – was that the disarmament fund could not do what it really wanted with respect to buying arms.

I think women were more inclined to put their necks on the line. They could take some risks with respect to getting out there in the street. You did not have that same thing from men of comparable status. They wouldn't want to put their necks on the chopping board like that. Another thing was the women could maneuver a little more than the men, going behind the scenes and trying to talk with people one-on-one and coaxing them as opposed to just being rigid. So I think women were a little more flexible and more courageous.

We were very fortunate to have a courageous leader in the person of Mrs. Mary Brownell because at the time it was risky to be taking certain stances with respect to peace. She was not the only one. It was an inspiration to work with a group of women who saw the need after a stalemate to create the Liberia Women's Initiative to see what they could do to advance peacemaking.

I learned [from a conference of International Alert, which brought together a number of countries that were in conflict situations] that we were not in this thing alone. And I found it very troubling that Liberians were fighting among themselves and that we had to go to another country to find a room even for us to talk. I remember that we did not talk with one voice over there. So, one of the lessons I learned was that I don't care how you go about it, you will have to sit down at some point to do some talking. The Liberian Women's Initiative, for example, initiated a project known as Bridges to Peace. For this peace thing you don't just rely on one strategy. Another very serious lesson I learned was that when women can work together for peace, then that ability can be translated to other situations. We can also work together for girls' education, for sex education of girls and so forth.

> When women can work together for peace, then that ability can be translated to other situations. We can also work together for girls' education, for sex education of girls and so forth.

To maintain this peace, we need to build on the democratic process that has started, to have mass education to advance the gains made by civil society during the war. We need to use the quest for peace as a rallying point to make a stronger civil society…. Because I am an educator, I think the school is a good, a very enabling environment for peacemaking and for reconciliation.

Weade Kobbah-Wureh, former Vice Chair, Council of State, Transitional Government (1996-1997)

One of the stories of my life I find very difficult forgetting is the story of the 1992 Octopus attack on Monrovia. I was then Director General of the Liberia Broadcasting Service. We had done enough work to know that an attack on Monrovia was imminent. Unfortunately, the peacekeepers felt otherwise. I remember talking to the then-chief of staff about reports coming out of Caldwell. His reaction to us was, "You Liberians like to believe in stories. Everybody is so paranoid that we need to allay people's fears, not to start stirring things up." General Bakut had ordered the backloading of all [West African peacekeeping] ECOMOG equipment because they believed sufficient discussion had been held with the NPFL, so there was absolutely no need to keep heavy weapons on the ground. [In addition] President Jimmy Carter had come saying President Taylor wanted peace but was afraid of all that heavy equipment of ECOMOG.

At the time we had the responsibility of monitoring the radio on the other side: our local language broadcaster kept translating things to us. When we heard people say on the air, "Look, the children we have no longer belong to us; they are being recruited or conscripted. So when you hear they catch some soldiers on this side, you go see if your little brothers are among them. We knew something was in the making.

ECOMOG equipment was practically nonexistent. I remember commuting between the Ducor [hotel where many members of the Liberian National Transitional Government lived] and the ECOMOG headquarters across the bridge, seeing the bullets flying, people running. I remember being in the ECOMOG headquarters when rockets were landing there. I remember...the bombing and breaking of the train tracks to stop the rebels coming into Monrovia. Monrovia was just about gone. Then we had to deal with 250,000 displaced people as a result of the attack.

What was needed was to open up another front and keep the pressure off Monrovia. And that is what we proceeded to do – to attract the NPFL away from Monrovia and allow the peacekeepers here to consolidate and secure the city. My satisfaction at the time stemmed from the fact that we were able to do exactly what we set out to do, which was to divert this attention for two-three weeks until the peacemakers could galvanize themselves, and beyond that to hold areas that we thought the interim government at the time would take over for administration.

That is one story that I find very difficult to forget, but that was the beginning of my involvement in military operations geared towards creating a leveled playing field for subsequent negotiations. It took its toll on my family life. And we had quite a few shortcomings: the principal one I remember was the attitude of the fellows I had to work with, their ability to be so full of themselves that they perceived whatever role I was playing as a man's role, and as such they had to dominate everything. But we were able to accomplish what we set out to accomplish. You have to prepare yourself for any repercussions of your actions. So when I had situations like people storming my house and trying to create the impression that it was full of arms and they needed to take the law in their own hands, I viewed it as one of those scare tactics: intimidate her sufficiently, and she will withdraw.

Liberia became a pie that everybody sought to divide in their own national interest, and ECOWAS in this whole process did not act as a single unit. That was another realization: a state's own interest will always supersede its involvement in another state. Liberia was just a country of competing interests. Everybody went to the negotiating table with their own agenda. Very rarely did the agenda have to do with Liberia. Hence it became important for those of us who were Liberians to chart an agenda that was solely Liberian. Focusing attention on Liberia was a key concern for me.

[During the negotiations] the men would strategize, yes. They would decide their positions, but they left very little room for negotiations. The women were more flexible and more tolerant. The men approached this whole issue as if they were arch enemies, but the irony was that, after, they would shake hands. The same people who were hugging and kissing each other here are at each other's throats. So those people who attempted to facilitate the peace could not distinguish between what actually led to the problem and why people were holding certain positions. If these people were all friends, why were they killing each other?

> Liberia became a pie that everybody sought to divide in their own national interest, and ECOWAS in this whole process did not act as a single unit.... Everybody went to the negotiating table with their own agenda. Very rarely did it have to do with Liberia.

Whenever there is a conflict situation the first thing to do is to try to negotiate. Try to discuss. You have to think about peaceful means of resolving conflicts because our experience has shown that "I spoil it, I will fix it" is not so easy to spoil and fix. Liberians believed that it was easier to make war and that with peace everything will flow. It does not flow that way. This is the bitter lesson we have to learn in Liberia that we all have to pay for those things we destroyed, whether they belong to other people or belong to the government. Hence, coming out of war we have found ourselves saddled with a lot of high taxes. We ruined school buildings; we'll pay heavy taxes on zinc and nails to get money to put back roofs. If we looted all the chairs out of public facilities, they will be put back through the pockets of every one of us. I think the lesson we've learned is not to get involved in violence because no conflict is resolved in violence. We're the least developed country in the whole west coast of Africa now…investors went elsewhere.

Theresa Leigh-Sherman, educator

My first experiences with peacemaking started after the 1990 war. We had been running during the war, afraid. Some of us set out to go to Sierra Leone where we stayed for a while. Then we started hearing that our parents had been killed – slaughtered. We came back to Liberia in 1991 with nothing. And

the war continued. Not long thereafter the women started grouping themselves, organizing into various NGOs. "What can we do? How can we make
these men (after all we are mothers), how can we make these men understand
that dialogue is better than the gun?" There were meetings and meetings and
meetings. Then we heard that they were having this summit in Abuja. They
[ECOWAS leaders and faction leaders] had been having a series of meetings
in Yamoussoukro [Côte d'Ivoire], Geneva, but this time we decided we wanted to be part of that meeting.

All the women were saying, "We must go to Abuja and meet the presidents
[of West African countries], the committee of nine." It was 1995. A position
paper was put together by all the women's groups. We met at the Planning
[Ministry] where it had been decided to send women to represent the women
of Liberia in Abuja. Of course we were not on the agenda, but we got to
Abuja. We had nothing but will power. We were proud to be Liberians, and
we felt it was time for the international world to hear our side of the story.

We went with our position paper. It was a serious paper because we did a data
fact finding. If we said the factions bombed a mosque in Cape Mount, we
gave the date and time. If we said a child was raped, we gave the place. It was
not a passionate thing; it was a factual position paper. But how to get there?
We just asked friends and we took collections, and that's how we bought our
tickets. Finally we got to Abuja.

We started lobbying in the hall for them to put us on the agenda the next day.
We met opposition: "I mean, lady, we understand what the women are suffering, but you are not on the agenda. This is a summit, an ECOWAS summit.
There are all nine presidents." We spoke with the president of Gambia, and he
said, "I will talk to…." We went to the special assistant to Rawlings [presi-
dent of Ghana and chair of ECOWAS at the time], who sent word in to
Rawlings that we wanted to present this paper. We went to Iroha [Nigerian
Ambassador to Liberia] and through Iroha we saw Ikimi [Nigerian foreign
minister] and they sent word for us to present the paper because Abacha
[Nigerian Head of State] was coming. We just touched base with all of the
presidents there at the time, and we presented our case. "We don't want jobs,
we don't want positions, we want peace. And the only way you all can decide
this is to hear what the mothers and the women of Liberia have to say. You're
listening to the factions, you have been listening to them. We bore them, we
carried them nine months, you should listen to us." They didn't give us any
guarantees, but I can bet you we did our homework for two nights. We just
lobbied and lobbied and lobbied.

The day of the conference we met in the hall in Nigeria, and it was decided that I would present this paper. We didn't expect it, but we prayed. Rawlings was presiding that morning. All of a sudden there was a break and we looked at each other. He [Rawlings] said, "Now ladies and gentlemen, we're going to deviate for the first time in ECOWAS. We have listened to the men, we have listened to all the factions, but we never listened to the civilians, we have never listened to our mothers, we have never listened to our sisters." We just grabbed each other's hands, we were shaking.... I took that piece of paper, I walked saying the 23rd Psalm and stood there and slowly talked [of the killing and atrocities] and of how we women were tired.

> We have listened to the men, we have listened to all the factions, but we never listened to the civilians, we have never listened to our mothers, we have never listened to our sisters.
>
> *President Jerry Rawlings of Ghana*
> *Presiding Chair of ECOWAS*

It was a 30-minute paper. We made recommendations. And I tell you the nine presidents that were there and the house of thousands of people – I'm talking about CNN, BBC, everybody – was in tears because these are facts that these people didn't know about, having heard the ordinary men on the street talk. But we have gone through it, we have lost everything we worked for.... So we had nothing more to lose but to tell them the truth.

And when I got through, I just took my paper and walked back. And the whole hall stood up and started clapping. The presidents, tears were in their eyes because they didn't know our side, and that turned the issue of Liberia around. They saw a different perspective of the war. They saw how we were suffering.

When we got back home, we got word that "You women, the factions are still at each other's throat. Can you all call them together and let them start speaking to each other?" All of the warring factions responded to our invitation to meet at the National Bank conference room. We met the factions, and we said, "Hey, my people, this is not the time for division. This is time for uniting. It is time to rebuild." When one man gets vexed and wants to walk out, we would run behind him: "My man, where are you going?" "That man said something," he would say. "Never mind. Just come back because this is Liberia we are talking about. It is greater than all of you."

At the end of the day they all became friends. At the end of the day we decided that we would come out with a resolution. We came out with a paper and all of them signed. We took this paper and handed it to the government. ECOWAS sent for the document because they couldn't get these people together. Only the women of Liberia could get all of these factional leaders together.

Elizabeth Sele Mulbah, Executive Director, Christian Health Association of Liberia

When the war came, we realized that a lot of people were traumatized and they needed healing. So at CHAL we established a healing and reconciliation department with the hope of addressing at least three basic professions: teaching, nursing and religious leadership. We wanted the nurses to be able to relate to their patients [often soldiers and abusers] in spite of whatever relationship they shared outside. If we didn't do that, patients would be afraid to go to the hospitals, for the nurses they met would be seen as enemies. We wanted the same thing done for teachers, so that once the war was over they would go back to the classroom, able to relate to students and teachers. Religious people should not condemn people; there is always a reason why people behave the way they do. So we wanted to work with the religious leaders to enable them to use their skills in religious reconciliation to bring people around.

The second time I became involved in peacemaking at the national level was when I was seconded to the United Nations Observer Mission to Liberia (UNOMIL). Here we brought tribal groups together, we brought civilians and fighters together. One very outstanding topic was "The ex-combatants coming home: What is in waiting? What are their expectations?" We divided participants into two groups: the civilians on one side and the fighters on one side. They discussed what each expected from the other. When they gave their reports the civilians said, "Look, these people came and deprived us of everything we ever had, they abused us. They have to come on bended knees to beg us." The reporters for the fighters were convinced that they came to liberate and therefore they should be given a heroes' welcome. The facilitators said, "Let's meet each other half-way." We told the civilians, "If you wait for these people to come on bended knees and say, 'We are sorry,' we may never have peace."

When I was with UNOMIL, we found out that each tribe in this country has a slightly different approach to reconciling a conflict. It may be very difficult for the criminal or the wrongdoer to be the one to come forward, so there is always a middleman who speaks and pleads on his behalf. If it is in the village, they will call the council of elders. If women are involved and it is serious, they are taken to their own village. Sometimes the middleman takes something like a kola nut. Depending on the level of the crime, it may be a chicken or even a cow, but it is presented on behalf of the wrongdoer, and once the chief of that town in consultation with the council of elders accepts that offering, it is split and shared among them. Hearts are mended and families are united as one.

One of the things I thought would have been useful during the time of demobilization was to involve our tradition. What I had hoped was that they would have taken the demobilized soldiers or fighters and symbolically turned over the power line to the council of elders. They could have brought a representative of the town chiefs and said, "The war is over. Here are your children; we turn them over to you." The chief would turn and say to the elders, "This is the request. Do we accept that?" And of course once the chief says yes, they all are going to say yes. They break up the kola nut and eat it. The main objective here is transfer of power, so that as of this date these fighters know that they now owe their allegiance to the chiefs, the council of elders, not to the heads of factions. But the way we did it – the modern way – fighters still maintained their chain of command to the heads of the warring factions. That loyalty was never broken.

What was important for us was that those who agreed to attend did get something out of the workshops. Their relatives had died and they had not even the time to mourn for them. So, one of the things we did was to take them through the whole process of mourning. There was a burying ceremony where you took something that symbolized your guilt, and we burned this at the end of the workshop. So people would come out and have an opportunity to cry. To see older men and women crying in these workshops was just moving.

But what used to happen during the workshops is that while we were talking about reconciliation, you turned on the radio during coffee break and heard there was an ambush or a riot and killings in the villages where some of the participants came from. We relived all the atrocities that they were trying to deal with! What is required is cessation of all hostilities and admission of guilt. Are we honestly prepared to tell one another, "I agree, I did wrong." That's the first step. Step number two: "I am sorry I did it." Number three: "Your attitude and your actions show true repentance." This is how true peace can be built.

> Are we honestly prepared to tell one another, "I agree, I did wrong." That's the first step. Step number two: "I am sorry I did it." Number three: "Your attitude and your actions show true repentance." This is how true peace can be built.

We had planned to do [these workshops for former combatants] in each of the political sub-divisions, and we had done 34 of them around accessible districts when UNOMIL was closing up.

The Liberian peace process, to me, is just starting. The reason I say that is, if you hurt me, let's say, you step on me and you are wearing a high heel and you say, "I am sorry," that only makes sense if I am no longer feeling the pinch. If you are no longer stepping on me, I am not feeling the pain anymore. But as long as you are stepping on me, and I am feeling it and you keep saying, "Liz, I am sorry," it's going to be very hard for me to swallow that.

Gloria M. Musu-Scott, Chief Justice

All through the war, I never left my country. I've never been a refugee, but I have been a displaced person. How did I get involved in the peace process? When I listened to the BBC on April 6, 1996, I heard that Liberians on the Bulk Challenge ship were turned away from one port and sent back onto the high seas because nobody wanted to accept Liberians. When my children asked why I was crying, I told them, "I am sure that I know almost everybody on that ship." In addition, I realized that our country had come to a point where Liberians were so desperate to get away from their own country that they boarded the worst ship you could think about – risked their lives just to get away. I prayed, "God, if you ever give me the opportunity to contribute to the peace process, I will do it."

One day in September 1997, I came to work and saw I was needed at the [president's] Mansion. When I got there I was told that I had been appointed Minister of Justice. I didn't really believe it. Then I thought, maybe this is the answer to my prayer. I just said, "Well, God, I know you will guard me because the issues are so large, the players are so powerful, and who am I to get involved in this thing?" I had never met Councilman Taylor who recommended me for the post. When we finally met he expressed shock because he thought I was some big old woman.

I was one of the founders of the Association of Female Lawyers of Liberia (AFELL) and its first president but had to give it up when I became Minister of Justice. Now, as Chief Justice I want to ensure that judges, magistrates, justices of the peace and even associate justices get better training to keep up with legal principles for our society. We also need to train the clerical staff – the clerks, the recorder – to know the implications of their work. Another goal is to have the law available to everybody in simple English, so that ordinary people can know their rights. For example, a woman who is in process of divorce or a person who's been accused criminally needs to understand the whole proceedings. I also want to set up an independent judiciary inquiry commission where people who feel that judges have arbitrarily gone outside the law or have taken advantage of them, can come.

It was during the elections that I got into the whole process. I came out of the Independent Elections Commission with more gray hairs than I went in; it was really nerve-racking. First the elections were postponed – a very fearful action because Liberians were restless and wanted the war to end so they could get on with their lives. We trained the poll workers. Registration was to commence on Monday, and on the preceding Friday the workers demanded their money before being deployed. We didn't have the money. It was a near riot. I almost passed out when the ECOMOG soldiers came to try to control the situation. Where would we get 6,000 persons to train between Saturday and Monday? That was the worst night I ever spent – I never slept. But the next morning I walked through the crowd, and the workers were saying, "We will go. We will work because of our country. We're tired of this thing. We want this war to end."

The opportunity was there for women to get into the national legislature, but we lost it. I never saw a political party with even five women candidates. Yet I must congratulate women...we're getting involved in political and national life, taking up opportunities that men have had for centuries. I'm happy that we continue to meet, to organize, to resolve our differences. We are doing it for the common good of women, for our children and grandchildren. Working with women has been a learning experience for me. I was a little sad when I saw our women's leadership problems appear in the newspapers, but I said, "What's going on happens in other organizations, and I shouldn't be sad because it's women this time." I think we need stronger loyalty. We shouldn't adopt the modus operandi of men.

I learned from our sisters in the Liberian Marketing Association who crossed the fighting lines with food to buy and sell. They could deal with ECOMOG, they could deal with the fighters. They kept Monrovia fed. Men had nothing to do with this – they were too fearful. When you talk to the women marketers you see their train of thought, their concepts. That shows me the importance of education, to allow such women reach their full potential. I say to myself, "If they were educated, they would move the world."

> Peace breaks down, in fact the whole system breaks down when people feel isolated, not appreciated, not contributing. There's nothing to keep them from destroying the system because they're not part of it. But when you create an atmosphere that everybody belongs, everybody contributes, everybody is important, you will contribute to the peace process. To build peace in Liberia involves everybody.

Several women inspired me: Golda Meir of Israel because at the time she was Prime Minister Israel was at war and a woman was leading. In our own times I heard of Angie Brooks Randolph, who made mistakes as all of us can. I hear she is still alive, but blind. Madam Suakoko was a powerful chief, one of the few women to have a Liberian town named after her. There are a lot of women who played their roles, like the nurses who took care of people, and the teachers who kept schools open. These women show that women can make it. I have always wanted to be a strong woman.

When there was a breakdown of our national fiber, people began fighting personal wars. You heard some say, "Oh, I was living with such and such person who ill-treated me. It was a time for personal vengeance. Peace breaks down, in fact the whole system breaks down when people feel isolated, not appreciated, not contributing. There's nothing to keep them from destroying the system because they're not part of it. But when you create an atmosphere that everybody belongs, everybody contributes, everybody is important, you will contribute to the peace process. To build peace in Liberia involves everybody, not just the leaders as most people think.

To be an effective peacemaker you must be a very patient person, you must be calm and a very, very good listener. You must listen not only with your ears but with your eyes. You must listen with your heart, your soul and your mind because sometimes people say one thing and they mean something completely different. You must be very slow to speak on what you hear.

It is my goal to contribute to an environment where there will be the semblance of justice, where the ordinary citizen in the street can have confidence in the chance to seek redress through the law and can settle controversies through an established process. As head of the Supreme Court I must ensure that when you take your controversy to the court, you will get justice, straightforward justice, transparent justice.

Martha Nagbe, farmer and businesswoman

I represent my businesswomen's organization in Gardnersville. We are farmers who grow okra, potatoes and greens. We used to have a four-acre swamp rice farm, then we bought 25 acres of land at Lofa Bridge, but during the time to harvest the rice the Mandingo people and Krahn people were fighting, so we ran from there. Since that time I never go there again. I never go to school, my mother na sent me to school. Since the war came, it's been rough on my husband, and I been taking all the activity of the business.

I'm still making my own farm. At least you have food to feed yourself, and you can employ people in this wartime. You will not pay them much, but you feed them three times a day. If everybody gets food, they will be satisfied. Human beings deal with food. You buy a cloth and use it ten years, but every minute you have to eat.

I started peacemaking in 1991. It was a community issue with misunderstanding between husband and wife. Then the factions started, everybody got their group: Johnson had his group, Kromah his group, then Boley, then Taylor. We women used to go around, we went to Gbarnga and met Mr. Taylor. "What you here for, women?" he asked. We explained, "You are a citizen of the country, so we come to you as Liberian women. We want peace. That is what we here for." We went to Johnson: "Johnson, you are a Liberia man. We the women are suffering. We depend on farm, on selling. If you don't sell, you can't educate your children. Look the way our children suffer, so we need peace." We left there, went to Boley, went to Massaquoi the Lofa Defense Minister. We told them: "You must leave the fighting and go to the ballot box. If you vote, the Liberian people will like you." Kromah voted, Boley voted, Liberia people na want them, so they could not carry them.

There were 13 county representatives went to Abuja with our leader, Chief Jalla Wolo. I was the only woman my county sent. I went as the only woman because women feel it, this war. Because the children who were dying were our children, we bore them. I say I will go there, go see the ECOWAS chairman and tell him how we feel in this country, we the women of Liberia. I was there the very day Ghana President Rawlings was leaving the chairmanship of ECOWAS and giving it to [Nigerian General Sani] Abacha. I went to Abacha, I spoke on behalf of my county that we want peace, we want disarmament, we want our children to go to school. Our country got out of hand. We beg you, we want peace. He say "OK." We presented a document.

I worked for peace with LWI, NAWOCOL, Women Action for Good Will, Concern Women – we all joined together to bring peace in this country. We went round from village to village to talk with those boys to put the gun down. We went to Po River, to Mount Barclay, to Lofa, even to the border. When the leaders were in town, we demonstrated on the streets: we wanted peace.

> We went round from village to village to talk with those boys to put the gun down. We went to Po River, to Mount Barclay, to Lofa, even to the border.... When the leaders were in town, we demonstrated on the streets: we wanted peace.

The hardest was when we went to Po River. They almost kill us. Those boys say no, they would not listen to us. But as mothers you can't give up. Ma Brownell led the group. Some time they want to do bad to us, almost naked us, but still you don't give up. You talk to them because they don't know what they was doing.

As all women we all pull together, we go to the church, we fast whole day, fast for peace. The Muslim too can go to the mosque and pray. We and the Muslim were together, all the women of Liberia. Evelyn Townsend, Musu Kemokai, Atan Molar, Ruth Perry and all. I went through hard times: my feet swelled up, no food to eat. I used to go in the swamp to pick meat, to drink the clear water.

You must keep on talking, you shouldn't give up. Every time you must tell your children they must put the gun down. You must make meetings, talk so the international world can come to your aid.

Ruth Sando Perry, Chair, Council of State, Transitional Government (1996-1997)

I was tired of war. I was tired of the killing of innocent citizens, destruction of infrastructure and people fleeing to strange lands. It was 1992, and I had just returned from medical attention when I met women forming themselves into groups to talk about peace, about disarmament before elections. We first organized ourselves as Women in Action for Goodwill, then later the Women's Initiative.

Women want peace in Liberia. We want the fighting to stop. We want the killing to stop, the destruction of property, the looting. We held peaceful marches involving all women – Christian women, Muslim women, rural women, women from all over. We wanted peace now and peace forever. We met obstacles and were criticized: people said on the radio, "Oh, those women are looking for jobs for their husbands and boyfriends." But that was not it. We were advocating to take arms away from little children, children who were abused.

A widowed mother of seven heading a household with 15 children, I was doing my business at home in Paynesville when we all ran from our homes to what we called safe haven, Logan Town. I returned in early August, and one day the old man who was setting up a reconciliation program, Chief Tamba Taylor, sent his boys to invite me to join his delegation to Abuja for the ECOWAS peace conference. Because this was what we women were advocating for, I agreed.

When I got to Abuja I was told my name was not on the list, so I couldn't be accredited. I explained that I could not have gotten on the army plane that took Liberians to Abuja if I didn't hear my name. The good Lord moves in mysterious ways: I happened on the Chief of Protocol, Paul Mulbah, who told me there was nothing he could do. Fortunately, about ten boys came along then, and they got documents. When Mulbah saw me he told the men, "This is a Senator." I got accredited but was determined to go to my hotel and not return to the conference hall to be embarrassed again. I was tired.

My roommate answered the phone – someone asking for Senator Perry. She repeated to the caller, "A Nigerian ambassador is waiting for her in the lobby?" I went to the lobby with a messenger who took me to a car, but I was afraid to get in. "Where am I going? I don't even know this ambassador." When I looked around I saw Counselor Cherude and asked if he would mind going with me. "I will follow," he said, and I said, "Oh my Lord." So I went, and that is how the whole thing started.

I was offered the task to head the transitional government as chair of the Council of State! I had to evaluate my very self: "Who is Ruth Perry? What can she do?" I felt the strength, the need, the willpower to take it. I decided first of all to pray, then to mobilize women because I felt this challenge was not for me alone – it was for the women of Liberia and all African women. I had to be neutral. I had to do everything possible not to let the faction leaders know that I was supporting anyone. My strategy was to be very firm but flexible with them. We had heated arguments on the council. Most of the time I argued for us to proceed, and most of the time they knew I was right. The main thing was to move into elections. When I was accused of making unilateral decisions, of handpicking people, I went before the chairman of ECOWAS to argue my case. He asked questions, then said I should go ahead because of the timetable given me.

Ruth Sando Perry

During the election campaign there were little problems and complaints here and there and yonder, but by then the Elections Commission had taken over. On the July election day the sky was gloomy and there were showers. There had been rumors of impending violence. People were in line from three or four o'clock in the morning until six-thirty in the evening just to exercise their franchise, their rights. It was the most peaceful election ever held anywhere around this continent. I was very happy. I probably made mistakes by not speaking out enough for educating the voters, so people had to educate each other. But we didn't make any big mistakes. Thank God for that. My success was an elected government.

After the inauguration I felt the need for rest, but I was asked to head a delegation to a conference on women, peace and development in Addis Ababa. While waiting to leave, ECOWAS and the OAU asked me to head a delegation to Burundi whose President Buyoya felt that his people, afflicted by ethnic fighting between Hutus and Tutsis, were suffering under international sanctions. People said it was risky to go there, but we went for an assessment mission and to mobilize women for peace as we did in Liberia. Asked to share my experience, I told them to find the root causes of their problem – whether external or internal forces – before they could find solutions. I knew that the root cause in Liberia was "We want to be in the president's mansion." If you want to be in the mansion, forget fighting, I said, and go to the ballot box.

We all know that African countries do not make guns. We don't make warlike materials. We take over our rich natural resources such as gold and diamonds, sell them and buy armaments to destroy our countries. For some time the Ivorian government had been stepping hard on us, passing arms through our borders. Guinea did the same. We had to tell those and other friendly

Photo courtesy of Elizabeth Mulbah

countries: Don't help us kill ourselves; help us to bring peace to our country.

What does it take to bring lasting peace to a country? Just a little touch of velvet and the stamina of steel. By that I mean you've got to be flexible, to listen, to hear, and be very firm with your decision-making. If you are not impartial you are not going to make it.

Marion Subah, nurse

What I could see in people was so much anger. People at the gates of Monrovia, people killing people. They were very, very angry. Everybody out there was their enemy. They were so angry they were irrational. If you asked them what they were doing, they would kill you. Some of us are now more aware of the injustices that were happening to people before the war, and the war was a response to all those unjust things.

People need to know there's nothing wrong with getting angry about injustice. You're supposed to respond to it. But how can we help people to show anger in a more peaceful way? How can we get people to be nonviolent? People should not say, "Me, I'm neutral" because if you are neutral, you actually agree with the people who carry out the killings.

Since 1991 the Christian Health Association of Liberia (CHAL) has been doing peace-building activities, workshops with different groups around the country. Before the war we worked with children to promote psychosocial care, but when the war came we started doing trauma healing and looking at ways for children to work through their situations and become peaceful. Then we did conflict resolution with fifth to twelfth grade students. We trained "palava [conflict] managers" as peer mediators between students. We've also had sessions with legislators. We have done workshops for chiefs and elders, about peace, about reconciliation. We have a program called "Peacemaking and Conflict Resolution in the Church."

A very big peace action I participated in was with the leaders of the fighting factions, a meeting at the National Bank. Women from LWI and WODAL and others came to CHAL and asked us to facilitate their session. The women's organizations called the faction leaders saying, "Please come, we want to talk before we go to Abuja." The first morning we met at the bank, we asked, "Why are you here?" and they replied, "When women like you call me, I will not come?" You know in Liberia men have a very great respect for their mothers, and if the mother says something they tend to do it. That is an advantage for us – if women themselves can become nonviolent people and listen to them. But if the mother says, "Go and fight," the person will go and fight.

We [Elizabeth Mulbah and I] went there with no agenda but took our peace story, operative games, the story of The Rainbow. Participants set the ground rules and decided the agenda. We led them at the beginning with our stories and games before they talked about their agenda. When we first started it was to be four hours, but then it went on for about four days. We went to help iron out disagreements and make some decisions before they went to the Abuja conference called by ECOWAS. After the four days we didn't think we accomplished much, but each day since then I see the things they decided in a particular meeting coming up: who would have what position, and how they would interact.

When I was growing up it was mostly women who marched and took social and political actions. But that has changed. If you go to Greenville to do a workshop now, you will find mostly men. When you go to communities for health care programs, you get the impression that it's the chiefs who decide. But the chief will say, "Well, you have to come back. I need to see my people." He goes, he sees the elders, the men, but he also sees the women. He gets a lot of information. The chiefs never say anything without consulting those women to get their ideas and come to a conclusion with them. And when you're there, you interact with the elderly women and realize very quickly that people come to them for information. Even though they act quietly and seem to be on the sidelines, they have an input to what happens to the community, just as they do in their houses.

Somehow in Liberia we need to establish a forum – something like the Truth and Reconciliation Commission in South Africa – where people who did terrible things can come out and say it, and ask for forgiveness. If people can work through the trauma, then we can start peace building. They have to grieve enough over the terrible things that have happened in our lives – either what we did or what people did to us – before we can really go forward.

Evelyn Townsend, Senator

After my husband was murdered in the 1980 coup I was bitter for a while, but you have to forgive and have a cut-off point for bitterness. I went to the United States for three years, then returned. My mother had died when I was seven, and the aunt who took me in made sure that I was educated right through college in London. When I came home I went to work at the Ministry of Foreign Affairs (then called the Department of State) and stayed there many years. We dealt extensively with the United Nations, briefing diplomats so that they could participate intelligently. I was involved in the Monrovia Conference where the OAU was evolved. Today I have from seven to 14 people in my household at any one time.

During the 1990-1996 conflict I was actively involved in the peace actions of Inter-Faith and Churches United for Peace (CUP) and women's groups. Heads of women's organizations, the female governors, the market women – all made significant contributions. Women's organizations came together (sometimes when we met there were 100 representing almost all women's organizations) and mandated several women to get actively involved in negotiations – to contact the opposing forces. We took a lot of risks. I went to Bomi right after ULIMO took over, when many people were afraid to go there. We had a very good meeting with their leaders, Nayou and Joe Harris, but as usual they said, "Go and talk to other factions." The women at grassroots were very, very useful – the market women for instance saw more of the combatants than we did. We asked them to tell the factions that destruction of lives and property doesn't benefit them or the nation.

It wasn't just women's groups. We worked with others to organize the All-Liberian Conference. You cannot separate the roles of citizens and say, "Oh, you're a woman" and "You're a man." You cannot develop a national plan or an organizational plan unless you get everybody involved. You have to have all views: men, women, girls, boys, every section of the community, then you can get a very good plan to build peace, to sustain peace. Nonetheless, I found that men would say, "We're going to fight." They were trying to be big and bad, be macho. Women were more compassionate, more objective. Mothers have sibling rivalry to deal with: all day you judge between children and you know the danger of making one child feel bad while the other feels right all the time. Women do everything to reach a good compromise.

Some of us have been everywhere there were peace talks. We went from Cotonou [Benin] to Abuja [Nigeria] – all the Abujas – to Accra, to Akosombo [Ghana]. The women mandated Theresa Leigh-Sherman, Mary Brownell, Clara d'Almeida and me to continue to hold talks with the opposing forces. Every one of the factions sat down together for the first time at the National Bank. The leaders laughed about being told "bedtime stories," but they just couldn't take their attention off the discussions. We built confidence before we started talking to them, so they believed us when we talked. They stayed four days! Then the ECOWAS ministers who were to meet in Monrovia came to us, saying we were the first to bring all factions together; they wanted our papers to use for their agenda.

The group came together to write a position paper to read at the mediation meeting, called Abuja I. We got ourselves there and couldn't afford separate rooms so got a single room with a very large bed. We just had to be there. We went to the ECOWAS Executive Secretary who was about to go to the airport to meet the then-Chairman, Jerry Rawlings. We wrote a small note together with our speech, and said, "Look, just give it to him and see what he says."

We heard no more. In the meeting, President Rawlings suddenly said, "Ladies, the floor is yours." I broke out in a cold sweat. Theresa Leigh-Sherman read our statement, and before she finished the heads of state were wiping their eyes, they were so moved by her presentation.

We took to the streets, we cried, we begged, we met in groups and said we wouldn't be satisfied until there was peace. Everything that was done towards peace was really influenced by women. First and foremost, we were out there demonstrating, passing out papers. We wrote to the wives of ECOWAS heads of state because that's the nearest head on the pillow, and they could talk to their husbands. We tried every trick in the book. We've been inspired by women's organizations in Zimbabwe, Uganda and a number of other African countries where women have stood up and gained influence.

Sometimes people insult you when you make the first approach; they don't want to hear what you have to say. Sometimes they call you deceitful or say, "Oh, you're just siding with somebody." They accuse you wrongfully. All the venom washes up on you. But what do you do? Hightail and get out of there? Or persist until you achieve the peace you have in mind?

Right now we have the problem of trying to overcome some of the societal ills that result from civil crises. People have old scores to settle, so it is important that we keep the peace process going – attaining peace is a process, it's not an event. The guns ceased, but we have to create the mechanism for peaceful growth. I'm committed to good governance and I will work day and night to achieve anything that brings credibility to this county.

> Attaining peace is a process, it's not an event. The guns ceased, but we have to create the mechanism for peaceful growth.

First and foremost I believe in dialogue. I don't believe in creating more factions to eliminate other factions. We've had NPFL that came to take Doe off our backs. We've had a proliferation of factions purporting to be "saviors" of Liberia. The whole country has suffered. Look around you at the destruction, at the collapse of economic activities and consequently of schools, of health clinics. Look at the prostitutes. You see children out in the streets making a living as breadwinners for their families. You see a huge soldier and a little girl maybe ten, twelve years old who is his girlfriend. Grown men running behind people's little children. That is child abuse. Maintaining the peace is the responsibility of every citizen.

Massa Washington, journalist

We have a parable about people who "have palm nuts in the fire roasting and want to get them out with bare hands." Obviously, you will get burned. But that is the tendency men have. They figure it should be hot, hot, cut steel with steel. They figure that a person should be punished by ostracizing him or denying him a job even if he's qualified. Women have a different, subtle approach. "No, we don't want any more fighting" or "Aha, man, people will continue to kill themselves." We employ a "softly, softly, catch monkey" approach. Try to pet the person, to coax him over.

I remember when the Liberian Women's Initiative started in February 1994. I was invited to help draft a position statement that would reflect women's views. It was my first major peacemaking activity, so when the statement was to be presented at the [government's executive] Pavilion I asked my editors if I might cover it. It was a very beautiful paper. Women called for peace, for a halt to hostilities. They were truly neutral. They said to the fighting men, "We are not backing any of you," even though some of their sons and other relatives were fighting. They were talking about the recalcitrant faction heads who refused to sign peace accords or would go to international meetings, enjoy themselves at the expense of the international community, sign peace accords then come back and say they were forced to sign, so that they could justify not adhering to whatever they signed.

At first the leaders thought the women were joking. But we were serious, we were stubborn, we were hardheaded. We all felt that the men had let us down because they were so prone to gravy-seeking. Yes, they do some nice things, but they have ulterior motives. You saw Ruth Perry, who chaired the Council of State. When it was time to step down, she stepped down without even thinking twice.

There were reactions in the media to our position statement at the Pavilion. The Minister of Posts and Telecommunications, Maxwell Kaba, was one of those who was very nasty towards it. He jumped up and said we were all frustrated women whose husbands had left us on the shelves, or were girlfriends of somebody in the interim government. The day after Kaba's story was carried in the newspaper I wrote a commentary on it, not really attacking him but being subtle and serious too. My article said, look, this war has happened, we've been marginalized for a long time. After six years of war, you've not given us peace. You cannot bring peace alone. We feel that it's time for us women to come in.

I represented LWI at two conferences [in 1994 in Ghana] that were prelude to the Abuja meetings. We wrote to ECOWAS that we the women wanted to be represented, but the men at the head didn't take us seriously. So we – Evelyn Townsend, Ruth Perry and others – invited ourselves to Accra. Interestingly, most of our benefactors were men in the private sector, in civil society. When ECOWAS and the UN, who were monitoring the peace process, ignored us the first day of the conference, we sat outside in the lobby of the conference venue like six cut-tail dogs. Each time there was a coffee break we would go to all those concerned, both warring factions and international community.

Prior to that, as soon as we got to Accra, I established contacts as a journalist with the Ghanaian and international press, including the Washington Post representative who was covering the event. So while the conference was going on, the women were already on the air and being quoted on local TV. We were also featured in the local newspapers. We got massive publicity. The international press asked, "Why can't they give the women a chance to participate?" On the second day we got observer status but weren't allowed to speak. During coffee breaks, we lobbied again: "You have to sign the peace agreement," we told everyone involved. On the third day we were granted official status.

> I established contacts as a journalist with the Ghanaian and international press. So while the conference was going on, the women were already on the air and being quoted on local TV. We were also featured in the local newspapers. We got massive publicity. The international press asked, "Why can't they give the women a chance to participate?" … On the third day we were granted official status.

We make mistakes in peace-building. Sometimes we assume that people don't know anything at all. That is because Liberians are maybe 85 percent illiterate, and we don't give them credit for what they are worth. But I tell you something: a person may not know how to read and write but that person may be smart. For me, the most important step to lasting peace is repentance. An elderly woman said to me, "The only thing I want is just for these people to say they are sorry for killing my son. They can't bring him back and I cannot demand they bring him back, but they can at least say 'sorry'." It could start with something like the South African Truth and Reconciliation Commission.

My father would tell us children: "Humans don't fight, it's cats and dogs that fight." He gave us the best education available at the time. I have a degree in Communications and English. Having fled Liberia several times there was fighting, I returned home, where my father and I are actually the heads of the household, of his younger children. Since the war I've lived in a lot of countries: Ghana, Nigeria, Togo, the Côte d'Ivoire, Rwanda, the States and Europe. Presently I work for the LWI as Information Officer.

The other day [an official] said the international community failed us. That kind of sweeping statement makes me want to take up my pen again and write actively: "Who failed you? Did they fail you? You failed yourself, as the people have said already. The Americans and the rest of them gave their criteria: 'We'd only come in if….' Now you are at the losing end. You've got a bad human rights record, you've got to straighten it up. And you've also got bad socio-economic policies. You say no, you can live in isolation and ignore all because you are big and bad. Have you heard of any country surviving in isolation? Even Hitler had allies in his war."

One way I would nourish and strengthen peace is to educate women. Look at the percentage of women in government in this country. If we decide to do things and we hold together, who can stop us? We've had women Paramount Chiefs and powerful people like Tetee Glapor who operated a Justice of the Peace Court using traditional methods, women who called people together when they thought there was conflict – even among children. They were very influential even though the men outnumbered them. They were always very strong and they did not have the benefit of a formal education. I would like to see women be more forceful; you have to be assertive so that people know you are serious. But people perceive women at the domestic level, no matter how bright they are.

Some people try to spread collective guilt, making everybody responsible for the war so they can get away with whatever they may have done wrong. I don't feel responsible for any war. Neither me nor my family have hurt anyone. I feel that eight to nine years of my life has been taken away from me; I wish I could get them back. I wish that we could be left alone in peace – to be free, to be able to get up in the morning and go to a job, to get paid at the end of the day. Peace means to be able to go to school, and if someone did you bad, to take that person to court and know that justice will take place. That's why I say "peace means life."

Conmany B. Wesseh, Executive Director
Center for Democratic Empowerment

In their search for peace, women used an approach that many of us did not have at first – a disarming personality and style. They were able to deal with the various armed factions when some of us didn't have patience. We men were so distrustful of the factions and their leaders that we didn't want to waste time talking with them, but the women kept going. They compelled faction members to want to listen. Their persuasiveness – laughing, joking about critical matters – got to the crux of things.

Through a new organization, the Liberia Women's Initiative, set up in 1994, they held separate meetings that brought faction leaders together. The meeting at the National Bank was ice-breaking. It was very critical since it came at a time of breakdown, of serious fatigue of everyone after the events of Akosombo where things went helter-skelter. Then there had been a coup attempt by [President Doe's chief of staff Charles "the butcher"] Julu, and Gbarnga had fallen…so when the National Bank meeting was convened, it was meant to bring together people to begin to see the folly of continuing fighting.

At a very critical moment after the Cotonou Agreement, the women contributed a great deal when we went on to Abuja [in May 1995]. They moved from one hotel to another, catching foreign ministers in hallways and compelling them to listen. Even those men claiming to be in a huge rush looked for a seat in the lobby to deepen the discussion or make an appointment. The next thing would be an appointment with one or another head of state. Then Theresa Leigh-Sherman addressed the summit on behalf of Liberia's women. Her passionate appeal for peace came through graphic descriptions of raping, killings, torture, exile, refugee life, the search for food – all that women had to suffer. The heads of state could not help but be moved by what she said and the way she said it. She contributed immensely to the decisions that arose from that meeting.

What I saw during the war was that women did a lot of consulting. They met with people in government and civil society, with faction leaders wherever they were. They talked to everybody. They presented themselves as mothers, mothers for all and mothers who were fair. I speak of the women – mostly members of the Liberia Women's Initiative – who were involved in making the peace, who as good mothers must be able to know when the child is wrong, when the child is pursuing a course of self-destruction and you show love for that child by raising issues of discipline. That is what makes women good peacemakers. They were criticized, but they were genuinely fair. Of course there were also some women who supported the war and even contributed to it, some as fighters.

That is the national level. But from my house or from my community I saw a lot of the peace-building efforts led by women. I guess they do it because their kids are always in the street and if there is a fight, they have to resolve it or find their beloved sons and daughters in conflict that might hurt them. So they make peace all the time. We hear about women trying to bring sense to bear among those who are about to unleash ethnic violence on each other. I guess this happens so often that we don't record it as major, but it is a significant part of daily lives.

Mary Brownell, the head of the LWI, was an effective leader of that group of women who used their own resources because there was no budget. She used her home for meetings. She was insulted by faction leaders because she emphasized that disarmament was the way to peace and those who wanted political power would have to disarm – no one should be allowed to take power through the barrel of a gun, through force. Women's organizations such as LWI, NAWOCOL and WODAL have built a national network of women peacemakers. LWI's Bridges of Peace project brings together persons of diverse background and opinion – political, religious, ethnic. That's a good thing, a good way to promote reconciliation.

We can have justice – political and economic – but to get it we have to stand up against injustice. We have to train ourselves, develop the capacity to recognize injustice and to show what is the law. You can't have reconciliation when those who commit crimes, sometimes very dangerous crimes, go around without remorse of conscience, without paying for their crime. At the moment women are holding important positions within the judiciary – the chief justice is a woman – and the police service. They can set an example with their work.

Peacemaking is about insuring that society operates on justice. It requires a great deal of give and take, to take account of the views, concerns and futures of the other party. The first important thing is to learn to listen to what the other side has to say, to put yourself in the shoes of the other side. One must not attempt to deal with all of the issues, but the key issues. In so doing you try to build from a small middle to a bigger and large middle with a capacity to absorb all, including the extremes. Then there is economic justice – the way by which we ensure that there is a fair distribution of the little that we have, that people can find jobs to take care of their families' immediate needs so that they can eschew violence and do those things that put bread on their table.

The first woman peacemaker I worked with was my wife. We agreed before returning to Liberia from exile in Ghana, where we were involved in social activism struggling for justice, that what we needed to do back home was try to build the peace, rather than seek to be government officials.

Annex 1:
BRIEF BIOGRAPHIES OF WOMEN AND OTHER PEACE ACTIVISTS INTERVIEWED
(current at time of interviews 1998-1999)

Mary Brownell was born in Maryland County, Liberia, educated in Liberia, and later attained a masters degree in the USA. A teacher and school principal, she is a founding member of the Liberia Women's Initiative, linking LWI with other Liberian civil society groups active in peace processes. She is a founding member of African Women for Peace.

Ruth Caesar was born in Margbigi County and educated in Liberia, Europe and the USA, up to an MA degree. She is Coordinator for Women and Children in the Ministry of Planning. She helped establish the Abused Women and Girls Project and organized support groups for displaced Sierra Leonean women.

Dorothy Musuleng Cooper was born in Montserrado County, gained an MEd in the USA and has been Academic Dean and Acting President of Cuttington University, Liberia. Under the LNTG government she was Minister of Foreign Affairs and currently is Chair of the Charles Ghankay Taylor Education Endowment and Humanitarian Foundation.

Etweda Cooper was born in Grand Bassa County and educated in Liberia and Europe. She has worked as a translator and run her own business and is currently the Secretary General of the Liberia Women's Initiative.

Clara d'Almeida was born in Maryland County and educated in Liberia before attending university and graduate school in the U.S. On her return she opened a school that she continues to manage. She was one of the small group that organized the mediation at the National Bank at the height of the conflict, and she attended the peace negotiations in Abuja.

Dorothea Florence Diggs was born in Montserrado County and graduated from the University of Liberia. Before her death in 2002 she was an administrative assistant at Star Radio. Her peace activities began through Lutheran church activities to assist displaced people and continued with her work for the Special Emergency Life Food Programme (SELF).

Elaine Dunn was born in Monrovia, graduated from high school in England and attended secretarial college in Liberia. She is currently employed with an investment company in Monrovia.

Kebbeh Freeman was born in Voinjama, became a businesswoman and member of the Liberia Marketing Association. She is superintendent and founder of the Redlight market and currently a member of the Liberian legislature. She cares for an extended family of more than 30 people.

Serena Galawolo was born in Nimba County and studied science and business administration at the University of Liberia. Driven from her home by the Doe death squad, she became involved in peace activities, promoting formal and informal mediation. She is currently a Vice Chairperson for the Charles Ghankey Humanitarian Foundation.

Hawa Goll-Kotchi was born in Bomi County, graduated from the University of Liberia and received an MA in the U.S. She is presently Secretary General of the National Commission for UNESCO in Monrovia. Her peace activities began in 1973 when she became involved with a human rights theatre workshop and continued through women's organizations.

Tiawan S. Gongloe was born in Nimba County and obtained a BSc in economics and a law degree at the University of Liberia. He is a well-known human rights lawyer and served as executive assistant to Amos Sawyer when he was president of the Interim Government of Liberia (1990-94). He is managing director of Legal Consultants, Inc.

Marie Kebeh Harris-Washington was born in Montserrado County, was not schooled as a child but enrolled in adult night classes. Currently Chair of the Board of Directors of the Liberian Marketing Association, she supports a household of 20 people including children, foster children and ex-combatants through her activities as a market woman.

Adama Jawandoh was born in Monrovia, received her elementary education in Sierra Leone and studied business at the University of Liberia. She is an Executive Member of the Inter-Faith Mediation Council and Vice President of the Federation of Muslim Women's Organizations. She participated in support activities for displaced people and mediation and peace advocacy.

Ellen Johnson-Sirleaf was born in Monrovia, educated in Liberia and received an MA at Harvard University in the U.S. She was Minister of Finance in Liberia, a World Bank officer and Assistant Secretary General and Regional Director of the Africa Bureau of the UN Development Programme. She was runner-up to Taylor in the 1997 presidential election.

Evelyn S. Kandakai was born in Monrovia, educated in Libera and attained a PhD in the U.S. During the war she chaired the peace education program of the National Adult Education Association of Liberia, working in schools and communities. She is currently Minister of Education for Liberia.

Theresa Leigh-Sherman was born in Monrovia and studied in Liberia and the U.S. She runs the Leigh Sherman Secretarial School and is currently President of the West Africa Women's Association. She remained in the country during the civil war and presented the women's statement at the Abuja peace meeting.

Wata Modad was born in Bolahun and studied at the University of Liberia. She helped set up the abused women and girls project with programs for women and children raped or otherwise traumatized. She is presently the Executive Director of the National Women's Commission of Liberia (NAWOCOL).

Elizabeth Sele Mulbah was born in Lofa County, educated in Liberia and gained a master's degree in nursing in the United States. She was the Primary Health Care Coordinator with the Christian Association of Liberia (CHAL) and started their Peace and Reconciliation Program.

Gloria M. Musu-Scott was born in Monrovia and educated in Liberia, graduating in law. A founder member of the Association of Female Lawyers of Liberia, she attended the Abuja peace negotiations and was a member of the Independent Electoral Commission. She is presently Chief Justice.

Martha Nagbe was born in Grand Kru. Without any formal schooling, she became a successful businesswoman and farmer. She was an active member of the Liberian Women's Initiative and traveled throughout the rural areas talking to combatants about disarming.

Ruth Sando Perry was born in Cape Mount County and educated in Liberia. She was Chairman of the Council of State in the Liberian National Transitional Government, achieving the mandate of disarmament, demobilization and national elections. She is a former senator and is involved in national and international women's peace activities.

Victoria Reffell was born in Sierra Leone, returning to Liberia in the 1960s with her parents. She studied journalism and has worked for the Monrovia City Corporation and the Liberia Broadcasting System. She currently chairs the National Reconciliation and Reunification Commission.

Amos Sawyer was born in Sinoe country, educated in Liberia and the U.S., receiving a PhD in political science. Former dean and professor of Liberia College at the University of Liberia, he was a founding member of the Movement for Justice in Africa and the Liberian People's Party, and former chairman of the Center for Democratic Empowerment. He was elected interim president and served four years as head of the Interim Government of National Unity (1990-1994).

Madam Annie Saydee was born in Sinoe County and attended elementary school in Eastern Liberia. She has been the Sarpo Governor in Liberia since 1984, was President of the Chadelly Women and was an active member of women's organizations during the war. She became President of the Rural Women's Association in 1997.

Maureen Shaw was born in Monrovia, attending elementary school in Liberia and high school in England. A businessperson, she currently runs a dressmaking and designing shop in Monrovia. Her involvement in peace activities began following the total destruction of her community through armed conflict. She was a founding member of the Liberia Women's Initiative.

Marion Subah was born in Greenville County, attended Cuttington University and studied nursing and midwifery in the U.S. Following a variety of positions in the nursing field in Liberia, she worked with children traumatized during wartime and is now Program Manager for the Christian Health Association of Liberia.

Evelyn Townsend was born in Grand Bassa County, educated in Monrovia and graduated from the University of London (U.K.). She has worked for the Ministry of Foreign Affairs and is currently a Senator. She was actively involved with the peace actions of Inter-Faith Mediation Council and the Churches United for Peace.

Massa Washington was born in Margibi County and received a degree in communications in Liberia. She has worked for the Ministry of Information and several Liberian newspapers. One of her greatest contributions to the peace process was in encouraging international press coverage on the exclusion of Liberian women at the Accra peace conference.

Deroe Weeks was born in Maryland County, graduated from the University of Liberia and gained an MA in the U.S. She was a prime mover in the counseling and rehabilitation work of the Abused Women and Girls Program and presently works on a USAID/UNICEF War Affected Youth Support Project.

Conmany Wesseh was born in River Gee County and is Executive Director of the Center for Democratic Empowerment (CEDE), a democracy promotion, peace-building and human security NGO. In 1996 he was special advisor to the President and later Minister of Youth and Sports. He is a founding member of International Action Network on Small Arms and founding Chair of the West African Action Network on Small Arms. He has been detained and exiled.

Tonieh A. Wiles was born in Montserrado County and attended high school in Liberia. After the 1992-93 Octopus outbreak she was forced to flee and spent many years working with refugee and displaced women outside of Liberia. She was actively involved in peace initiatives through her church and was a founding member of Women in Action for Good Will.

Vivian Titi Wreh was born and educated in Monrovia and attended graduate school in France. She worked in the Ministry of Foreign Affairs, eventually becoming Deputy of Protocol for the Head of State, Ruth Perry, after brief stays in Guinea and Ghana where she worked with refugees.

Weade Kobbah Wureh was born in Monrovia, attended school in Liberia and pursued graduate studies in broadcast journalism in the U.S. She was the Executive Director of the Liberia Refugee, Repatriation and Resettlement Committee and currently lives in Ghana. She helped use radio to establish dialogue among different factions in the conflict.

Annex 2:
LIST OF INTERVIEWERS

Davidetta Brown, Lansana senior program producer and assistant manager, Star Radio

Rufina Darpoh, gender and peace-building officer, Center for Democratic Empowerment (CEDE)

Edith Gongloe, reporter, Star Radio

Musue Haddad, reporter, photojournalist for News newspaper

Elizabeth Hoff, Enoyi producer, Talking Drums Studio

Barbara Koffa, producer, Talking Drums Studio

Medina Wesseh, coordinator of the women's NGO network and executive director of the Women Development Association of Liberia (WODAL)

Annex 3:
SELECTED FURTHER READINGS

Adebajo, Adekeye, *Building Peace in West Africa: Liberia, Sierra Leone, and Guinea Bissau,* International Peace Academy, New York, 2002.

Alao, Abiodun, John Mackinlay and 'Funmi Olonisakin, *Peacekeepers, Politicians, and Warlords: The Liberian Peace Process,* United Nations University Press, Tokyo, 1999.

Anderlini, Samam Naragbi, *Women at the Peace Table: Making a Difference,* United Nations Development Fund for Women, New York, 2000.

Association of Concerned African Scholars, "Women and War" in *ACAS Bulletin,* No. 55/56, Spring/Summer 1999.

Bennett, Olivia, Jo Bexley and Kitty Warnock, Eds., *Arms to Fight, Arms to Protect: Women Speak Out About Conflict,* Panos Publications, 1996.

Burke, Enid de S., Jennifer Klot and Ikaweba Bunting, *Engendering Peace: Reflections on the Burundi Peace Process,* African Women for Peace Series, Primex printers Ltd., Nairobi, 2001.

Dirasse, Laketch, "Gender Issues and Displaced Populations," in Heyzer N., S. Kapoor and J. Sandler, eds. *A Commitment to the World's Women*, pp. 214-225, Women, Ink, New York, 1995.

Dirasse, Laketch, "From Crisis to Transformation: A Gender Analysis of Conflict," in *Development and Gender in Brief*, No.3, IDS Sussex, 1996.

Fitzgerald, Mary Anne, *Throwing the stick forward: the impact of war on Southern Sudanese women*, UNIFEM & UNICEF, Nairobi, Kenya Litho printers, 2002.

Fleshman, Michael, "African Women Struggle for a Seat at the Peace Table," in *Africa Recovery*, Vol.16, No.4, February 2003.

Houten, Helen Van, and Zewdineh Beyene, *Placing Gender in the Mainstream* (Proceedings of the IGAD Policy Seminar on Peace Building and Conflict Resolution), IGAD & UNIFEM, Djibouti, 2001.

Machel, Graça, *A Critical Analysis of Progress Made and Obstacles Encountered in Increasing Protection for War-Affected Children*, UNIFEM & UNICEF, C. Hirst & Co. (Publishers) Ltd., United Kingdom, 2001.

Machel, Graça, *The Impact of War on Children*, UNIFEM & UNICEF, C. Hirst & Co. (Publishers) Ltd., United Kingdom, 2001.

Mulei, C., L. Dirasse and M. Garling, eds., *The Legal Status of Refugees and Internally Displaced Women in Africa*, Space Sellers Ltd., Nairobi, 1995.

NGO Working Group on Women and International Peace and Security, *Security Council Resolution 1325: Two Years On,* NGO Working Group, 777 UN Plaza, New York, 2002.

Rehn, Elisabeth and Ellen Johnson-Sirleaf, *Women, War and Peace: The Independent Experts' Assessment on the Impact of Armed Conflict on Women and Women's Role in Peace-Keeping*, UNIFEM, New York, 2002.

Turshen, Meredeth and Clotilde Twagiramariya, eds.. *What Women do in Wartime,* ZED Books Ltd., London, 1998.

UNIFEM, *Engendering Peace: Reflections on the Burundi Peace Process*, New York, 2001.

UNIFEM, *Somalia Between Peace and War: Somali Women on the Eve of the 21st Century,* New York, 2001.

UNIFEM, *Sudan Between Peace and War: Internally Displaced Women in Khartoum and South and West Kordofan*, New York, 2001.

United Nations Division for the Advancement of Women, "Expert Group Meeting on Political Decision-Making and Conflict Resolution: the Impact of Gender Difference," United Nations, New York, 1996.

United Nations Security Council, "Report of the Secretary-General on women, peace and security," S/2002/1154, United Nations, October 16, 2002.